DARK FORCES

A COLLISION OF TWO WORLDS

MARTIN REGINALD GRIMES

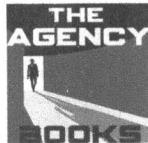

THE AGENCY BOOKS

an imprint of Sunbury Press, Inc.
Mechanicsburg, PA USA

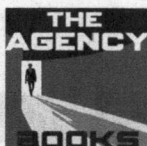

an imprint of Sunbury Press, Inc.
Mechanicsburg, PA USA

For information about special discounts for bulk purchases, please contact Sunbury Press Orders Dept. at (855) 338-8359 or orders@sunburypress.com.

To request one of our authors for speaking engagements or book signings, please contact Sunbury Press Publicity Dept. at publicity@sunburypress.com.

FIRST AGENCY BOOKS EDITION: May 2023

Set in Adobe Garamond Pro | Interior design by Crystal Devine | Cover by Lawrence Knorr | Edited by Lawrence Knorr.

Publisher's Cataloging-in-Publication Data
Names: Grimes, Martin Reginald, author.
Title: Dark forces : a collision of two worlds / Martin Reginald Grimes.
Description: First trade paperback edition. | Mechanicsburg, PA : The Agency Books, 2023.
Summary: *DARK FORCES* embarks on a voyage of unintended consequences that begins with honorable intentions. The author, highly skilled in complex financial investigations, ultimately represents clients who are money launderers and steeped in the art of international intrigue and economic/political assassinations.
Identifiers: ISBN : 979-8-88819-114-9 (paperback) | ISBN : 979-8-88819-115-6 (ePub).
Subjects: TRUE CRIME / Abductions, Kidnappings & Missing Persons | TRUE CRIME / Espionage | TRUE CRIME / Organized Crime | TRUE CRIME / White Collar Crime.

Product of the United States of America
0 1 1 2 3 5 8 13 21 34 55

Continue the Enlightenment!

TO ALL THE BRAVE MEN AND WOMEN
OF UKRAINE WHO ARE EXPOSING
THE VILE AND EVIL CRIMES
SANCTIONED BY VLADIMIR PUTIN

CONTENTS

AUTHOR'S WARNING

This narrative is based on a tiny sliver of history after the collapse of the Soviet Union and will demonstrate that regardless of how well-intentioned your motives may be, a world of unintended consequences can quickly consume you.

The artificially-compressed events in this incredible journey are actual. Journalistic liberties have been taken, camouflaging the true nature of the experiences or conflating the identity of the person(s) but remaining true to their essence. Out of privacy considerations and not wishing to humiliate or provoke those who were part of this journey, I have resorted, in most cases, to pseudonyms. Any remarkable similarity to actual persons, living or dead, is purely coincidental.

I have re-created the dialogue between myself and the various characters as these conversations best reflect my memory. Fiction and reality often are one big blur. There is that which we see and that which a "bodyguard of lies protects." Rest assured, what confronts you is a world of craven greed, clever deceptions, and an internal security apparatus that wears many treacherous masks.

Russia was the wild west in the 1990s and until the mid-2000s. It was out of control. Dystopian to some. Like the Roaring Twenties, money was flowing. It was a roller-coaster ride for those fortunate and courageous enough to navigate this utter madness. Globalization was the future—or at least that's what I thought.

If you walk away with nothing more from this adventure, never forget:

Today you may be on the side of the angels
Tomorrow you are dancing with the devil
Both are intoxicating
Both can be lethal

THE SCENE: 1994-2001

It was Christmas of 1991, the last day the Soviet Union ceased to exist. A Commonwealth of Independent States emerged from the rubble, with Belarus and Ukraine as part of this new world order. "The Soviet Union as a subject of international and geopolitical reality no longer exists," Mikhail Gorbachev, its president, announced. It culminated in the reforms Gorbachev introduced when the Berlin Wall fell in 1989.

There was an economic and political restructuring of Russia. The terms *glasnost* (political openness) and *perestroika* (economic restructuring) described this new geopolitical reality, as did the emergence of strategic corruption on a grand scale.

Gorbachev resigned from the presidency. Inaugurated as Russia's new president was Boris Yeltsin. Capitalism replaced communism. It was a time of both economic and political turmoil.

The movement of illicit goods, the provision of illegal services, extortion, brutal assaults, and murder became commonplace, part of Russia's nomenclature.

I entered this violent world, conducting due diligence on behalf of Russian clients. It was another journey into the abyss. It led me to conclude that the upper world was merely a creature of the underworld.

It also convinced me that the Soviet Union of the past was about to transform into a towering geopolitical criminal enterprise, unrestrained by international boundaries or laws.

Today, we are witnessing that transformation.

CAST OF CHARACTERS

---

* Lawson, Jack. 2009. *Slaver's Wheel: A Green Beret's True Story of His Classified Mission in the Congo.*

Gregori	KGB, Moscow
Golubev, Yuri	Absconded with $100 million from Russian Income Bank
Guisipinna	Investigator, Prague
Illif, Roman	Brighton Beach Gangster/Mob Boss
Ivanov, Peter	Berman's Partner, KGB
Joan Summers	Maxim's Manager
Kaminsky, Joseph	WWII Belarus Patriot
Koslov, Natasha	Bank Vice President; Bankers United Bank, NYC
Kostigan, Ivan	Latvia, Investor
Krupin, Vladimir	Latvia, KGB
Lithkov, Alexander	Owner of Taxi Companies
Lukashenko, Alexander	President, Belarus
Matteo	Investigator, Prague
McComb, Jack	CIA, NY
Molchalin, Gennady	Director, Russian Income Bank
Marisha	Paramour, KGB; Moscow, Prague
Oleg	KGB, Prague
Olga	Paramour, KGB; Moscow
Peterson, Robert	Husband of Natasha Koslov
Palmisano, Anthony	Former CIA; Investigator, NYC
Persico, Sal	Attorney, NYC
Portonosky, Ivan	Priest, Brighton Beach
Powis, Maximillian "Max"	London, Investor
Pullman, Tony	London, Private Investigator
Putin, Vladimir	President, Russia
Rappaport, Roger	Attorney, Denver
Rockoff, Dimitri	Moscow, Investor

Rockoff, Simon . . . . Moscow, Siberia, Mining
Executive
Rogov, Boris. . . . . KGB; Electrical Engineer,
Berman's Partner
Rostov, Gennady . . . . Russian Money Launderer
Rosenstein, Boris . . . . Currency Trader, Moscow
Rukonokov, Sergi . . . . Russian defector
Savage, Michael . . . . Former NYCPD Detective
Shasha . . . . Gregori's wife, Minsk
Summers, Joan . . . . London, Maxim's Casino
Summers, John. . . . . Former Scotland Yard Detective
Tanya . . . . Wife of Boris, Moscow
Tolstoy, Alexandra . . . . Putin's Banker's Paramour
Valery. . . . . Former organized crime
investigator, Minsk
Victor. . . . . Investor in Colorado Real Estate
Yelstin, Boris . . . . Former President of Russia

PLACES/INSTITUTIONS

Andaz Hotel. . . . . Prague
Babbo. . . . . New York City
Baden-Baden Casino . . . . Germany
Bankers United Trust . . . . New York City
Brighton Beach . . . . Brooklyn, NY
Caribou Club. . . . . Aspen
Casino de Monte Carlo . . . . Monaco
Claridge Hotel . . . . London
Eurokral. . . . . Moscow, Riga, Kiev
Friedrichsbad Baden-Baden . . . . Baden-Baden
Grand Hotel. . . . . Prague

THE BEAR AWAKES

"Mr. Gorbachev, tear down this wall." Ronald Reagan, in 1987, admonished the former Soviet Union leader, Michail Gorbachev, to remove the rebar concrete wall that separated East and West Germany. It was a defining moment in geopolitics and, in some respects, ended the Cold War. But was it? Or did another Cold War emerge that unleashed financial greed in the United States and Russia?

The globalization of crime and, more specifically, organized crime has now taken on a new dimension. Borders were open to financial markets that once were closed to foreign investment and exploitation. The Russian stock market became a unique investment tool for money launderers worldwide. Connecting to the Kremlin afforded exclusive control over industries the Russian government once owned. "Oligarch" became synonymous with a gangster, racketeer, and robber baron.

These were high-octane times, with money transferred through western banks to real estate moguls, manufacturers of yachts and private aircraft, and the world of rarified art. The lives of these oligarchs, their wives, mistresses, children, and grandchildren decades from now were instantly and substantially changed.

Suddenly, a new wild west had opened up to the Western world with the advent of unrestricted travel. Those with the courage and audacity accumulated *wealth* as opposed to money. They *competed,* perhaps an oxymoron, in a world with few rules. The overarching ethos was secretly investing in safe havens. There were no guardrails, providing you had a *krysha* (i.e., roof)—someone who would run interference for you to prevent or mediate trouble.

My friend, Igor, was intimately involved in the import-export business in Belarus, one of the few remaining European dictatorships. To run a business in Belarus, you had to pay off those who owed their positions in government to its dictator, Alexander Lukashenko. Every shipment into Belarus would be accounted for to ensure Lukashenko and his cronies received their cut. We are talking about millions of dollars in payoffs that have never seen the pages of a spreadsheet—at least not a legitimate one. Through Igor, I learned the dark side of the business in the former Soviet Union and became associated with many of his nefarious partners.

Igor was far from this Russian oligarch featured in magazines or tabloids. He was, in many ways, non-assuming, living relatively modestly and raising a family. His wife was an accomplished physician who could not practice in the United States because of the differing requirements in medical training. Igor was content driving a Toyota instead of a Mercedes, vacationing in the mountains of Iceland or Patagonia in rather spartan hostels. He led an unassuming life in a sleepy bedroom community. To Igor, wealth was a whisper, not ostentatiously promoted or displayed. Having spent a considerable time in a Belarusian prison, Igor learned that unless you had a *roof*, doing business in Belarus was chasing fools' gold.

Igor's run-in with the law was that he failed to pay off those who allowed him to do business in Belarus. Cheating your benefactors resulted in imprisonment. The notion of a fair trial or appeals to a higher court was alien to this newly-formed government which labored under the relics of the Communist Party. After paying over a quarter million dollars to be released, Igor learned his lesson. Your license to do business in Belarus was applying lubrication to the bureaucratic hurdles that made ethical business practices impossible. Your money was their money. So long as the gears are greased, there were no breakdowns in the production line. It was a simple equation that Igor understood, having been a chemical engineer before becoming an entrepreneur.

When I first met Igor and his wife in Minsk, I shared dinner in their rather well-appointed and spacious apartment—certainly quite luxurious by Belarussian standards. The walls had bookshelves everywhere, which addressed the history of the Soviet Union, the political philosophers who became icons to the Russian people, and the cultural institutions that made Russia a pre-eminent tourist destination to the art lovers of the Western world. There were books by Dostoevsky and Tolstoy, art by Rublev and Rokotov, and music by Stravinsky echoing through the apartment. Igor was, in many respects, a renaissance man, shaped and contorted by a corrupt and evil regime that had no respect for the fundamental democratic principles that brought some legitimacy to the rule of law.

Understanding this complicated yet charismatic human being intrigued me. My fascination to untangle the influences in his life that permitted him to rationalize his own (mis)behavior and that of governments was part of decades-long inquiries into those who roamed and flirted in the underbelly of society.

Igor's curiosity allowed him to opine on what I and many others would view as a most cynical take on the government. Igor had little to no faith in government for or by the people, words he dismissed as western fairy tales. In Igor's view, the government was simply a means to extract from its people human capital—a classic socialist and, to some, communist perspective.

Those who understood this and attempted to break the chains that imprisoned the human spirit known as freedom was labeled gangsters, racketeers, and now oligarchs. Freedom to Igor was the right and ability to engage in a business with little to no government interference. It was the right to speak your mind with no government censorship. It was the right to accumulate wealth with little to no government expropriation. He was the quintessential libertarian who saw government as an obstacle to equality instead of a moderator of inequality.

Knowing Igor added to my portfolio of underworld sources, although I did not see him in this somewhat villainous light. Igor was simply a Russian businessman making a rather well-deserved living, playing by the rules of a corrupt system. It made him no more or less a criminal. As Igor would often say, "a criminal is those who refuse to conform to the rules that take from the state what the state believes it deserves." Igor was certainly wedded to an ideological framework that saw little value in government other than perhaps protection from foreign invasion.

Of course, this made Igor the rogue that captured my interest. He saw the world inverted to what I believed. He reminded me of my first encounter with a Russian defector.

Ruminating with Sergi Rukonokov, I was fascinated by his command of the English language. His willingness to share the secrets of his life as a spy for Russia was breathtaking.

"Why," I would ask Sergi, "did you decide to defect to America?"

He answered, "I wanted my family to have a better life than I had." It was the definitive answer that followed me throughout my international forays.

In the mid-80s, my only knowledge about Russia and the Soviet Union was what my parents told me or what I "learned" in school. I had relatives who lived in East Germany, and periodically I would hear horrible stories about the Stasi and how cruel and barbarian the Russian government was. Of course, I now realize that this was the government in which Vladimir Putin played a significant part as a KGB agent.

Sergi was more than forthcoming. He related to how the FBI treated him as opposed to the CIA. He felt that the FBI had better skills in dealing with defectors than the CIA, "who looked down upon them for betraying their country . . . The FBI agents I dealt with understood what I was psychologically going thru . . . they made an effort to ease my transition into your country . . . whatever I asked for, they ensured I got it . . . the CIA agents were not as welcoming. . . ."

As we spoke, I could feel the trepidations that Sergi must have encountered, especially since it was difficult not to see himself as a traitor. To turn on your country, especially a world power, had to be a tortuous decision.

In one of the more humorous conversations with Sergi, he ruminated about being stationed in Somalia. "Sitting around the table with several representatives from various countries, all were there on behalf of the Red Cross. As they were excessively imbibing in spirits, primarily vodka, it became increasingly apparent they were all spies on behalf of their respective countries. They all began laughing as they knew who the other spies were . . ."

When I queried Sergi, why the Red Cross? His response was straightforward. "What other agency can go anywhere worldwide with no questions asked?" My naivete was embarrassing. But it taught me the value of a "beard" when I traveled to these communist countries.

Yet Sergi, much like Igor, was contemptuous of their government's treatment of their people. In the end, neither saw little hope for the future. Both chose a path that led them from the shackles imposed upon them by their respective authoritarian governments. America was a dream come true, even though it has never been overly receptive to immigrants.

What I like to call the dark side, breaking into this world, was not easy. Nor was it all that safe. Not knowing the language was a severe impediment. Understanding the body language of a foreign culture proved quite challenging. And eating and drinking with defectors, some of whom were KGB agents or informants for the KGB, always made me uneasy. Surely if they could lie, cheat, and inform their government, their allegiance to me would be non-consequential.

Fortunately, my years investigating organized crime and corruption served me well. "Keep your friends close and your enemies closer" was a phrase that echoed endlessly in my head.

Similarly, the Russian oligarch's "seldom personal, always business" found its way into their underworld's literature. I realized that if I were ever to grasp the social nuances of this emerging subculture, I would have to rely upon my earlier exploits investigating the Mafia's subculture. Over time, however, I realized that the more that was the same so much was significantly different.

The Russian oligarch, for example, monopolized entire industries, most of which were Russia's natural resources; they were usually highly educated and unquestionably well-cultured. They did not evolve from an agrarian culture but were a product of a highly accomplished educational system that promoted the physical sciences. The oligarch acquired a taste for the finer things in life, if through nothing other than osmosis. Art, of course, was one of the luxuries that proved a means of acquiring both status and wealth and an avenue to launder money obtained illegally. These were stark differences.

Moreover, the oligarch's political interest was to promote his business or entrepreneurial interests. Currying favor with the Kremlin's strongmen or men through partnerships and payoffs was the cost of doing business. To the Russian oligarch, the Foreign Corrupt Practices Act was a joke. It ignored the actual cost of doing business in the real world. It promoted the financial interests of American tycoons vis-à-vis oligarchs. As Igor would often say, "why is what we are doing any different from what Rockefeller, Morgan, Ford, or Carnegie did? . . . Or Donald Trump?"

This dialogue naturally led me down that crooked path to question the arbitrary construct between organized crime and white-collar crime. Igor viewed America and its puritanical, Protestant ethic beliefs as an outsider—someone who could distinguish the forest from the trees. On the other hand, I played the game as an insider, believing there were distinct and identifiable differences between those in the underworld or the dark side and those in the upper world—the political elites. Simply put, the forest was synonymous with the trees.

Again, fortune is often the residue of design. Having studied under several far-left criminologists from Great Britain, a country where social class is ingrained in your DNA, it was apparent that Igor and Sergi were parroting the classic *Crimes of the Powerful* argument. It was my opening to ingratiating myself to their world. It allowed me to shed the perennial view that "anybody can rise to the presidency" and embrace their point of reference.

Perhaps there is very little difference between the dark or opaque side and the light or transparent side? Both deal in euphemisms, clichés, and words. Nonetheless, the proof is in the pudding. The accumulation of wealth and the erosion of class and privilege are the consequences of a free market that rewards meritocracy. Igor and Sergi understood this equation. It's what bonded me with Igor and Sergi as I entered their world in my country.

While both Igor and Sergi were reluctant to share too much with me, particularly involving their relationships with what they referred to as their handlers or *roofs*, the passage of time has a way of chipping away at the rough edges, smoothing a path into their world. Before long, I was invited to dinners with them in New York's Little Italy, Tribeca, Mid-Town, and the Upper West Side.

Their handlers from Russia usually accompanied them. Introduced to the handler as someone they could trust, I knew, as did they, that trust was fleeting. While the handler would only speak his native tongue, denying being conversant in English, I certainly knew better. The handler was a man of few words. He just listened and stared. To use the term daunting or bone-chilling would be an understatement. I was entering a world I relished for its intrigue and adventure.

Fortunately, my relationship with Anthony Palmisano, a former CIA operative who laundered money in Latvia for business people and KGB informers, provided me with an ongoing tutorial on what to look for and expect. It also gave me a sense of security as I often exchanged my experiences with him.

Nonetheless, I also realized I was on my own, no longer having the protection afforded me through my law enforcement credentials. This was a whole new world in which deceit was the overriding ethos. Fortunately, my street instincts prevailed.

Whether excursions in New York City or Atlantic City, overnight train rides from Moscow to Minsk, and time spent in Prague, London, or Monaco with a former KGB agent, the experience proved once again "never under-estimate the power of the invisible hand."

Hopefully, this will open your eyes to how our current *knowledge* masquerades as *authentic history*.

Or, to paraphrase Paul Simon, "when I think back on all the crap I learned in high school," I now realize just how misinformed I was!

TIME—THE GREAT MEDIATOR OF HISTORY

Few things in life are etched in stone. Indeed, history is <u>not</u> one of them. As time progresses, so does our understanding of past events, events that at the time usually meant something other than what they mean today.

When I initially entered the private sector, it was when the Iron Curtain isolated the citizens of the former Soviet Union from the western world. My knowledge base was stories often told by spies, dissidents, social activists, or defectors who gave us a peek into this closed society. There was no internet, social media, cell phones, Twitter, Instagram, or Facetime. Long-distant calling was expensive and spotty, assuming you had someone to call in the Soviet Union. Perhaps even the term isolated is a generous euphemism for imprisoned. What we learned from our teachers, peers, and rudimentary writings defined our knowledge of this dark and alien culture.

I was fortunate to have relatives who lived in East Germany in some respects. After the war, they lived under Russian rule until East and West Germany were reunited. They bought into the communist ideology for no other reason than to make a living for their family. To this very day, they remain devout East Germans, suffering from relentless indoctrination denigrating Western values.

Growing up under the never-sleeping-eyes of the Stasi was, if nothing else, a nerve-wracking experience. Paranoia is the mental consequence of never knowing who might be the next informer to turn you in for some minor indiscretion translated into a security breach or threat. There is no doubt about the psychological costs of living under authoritarian governments.

Freedom to voice your objections to the government's policies and actions and demonstrate and associate with those who may be less than worthy in the eyes of their government is a fragile human right—as is democracy.

The rule of law ingrained a healthy and generous respect for human and civil rights and could channel the avaricious greed of the human condition. It was the answer to a society that equated privilege with wealth. With all its geopolitical implications, the fall of the Soviet Union failed to understand this delicate equation. Crime on a global scale became the defining characteristic of this welcomed yet untested implosion.

Transnational crime was a term that captured the imagination of criminologists in the 1990s. Then, I entered the private sector and began a career as a private investigator. Unlike that often portrayed in movies such as *Magnum PI*, private investigations often involved plenty of interviews and surveillance. The term "gumshoe" was a common phrase depicting the private eye who did a lot of walking and, in the process, collected a lot of discarded gum on the soles of their shoes.

With the introduction of corporate intelligence in the 1990s, an entirely new genre of investigative services was born. Many of which were engaged in mergers and acquisitions. Corporations relied on the information collected by analyzing 10K's and 10Q's and interviews with current and prior employees. It proved to be a lucrative money-maker for those entering this field of investigation. And if the timing is any predictor of success, it was at the time in my career that I welcomed a change.

Having attended several conferences at Cambridge University in the 1980s and 1990s, I was influenced and educated by the academic giants studying transnational crime. Once again, it proved to be an exhilarating and captivating experience, and the timing proved prescient.

Attending these international conferences also allowed me to visit colleagues I had worked with at Scotland Yard. The investigative function was undergoing a metamorphosis. Transnational crime was the flavor of the day.

As London was the financial capital of what would become the European Union (EU), more and more money was *invested* in real estate. Those who had access to the power structures of the sleeping bear— the Kremlin—were extracting capital from this untapped resource and *investing* (i.e., laundering) it through opaque real estate acquisitions in London.

These relationships, both in the academic community and among the practitioners, allowed me to expand my knowledge base from domestic organized crime to one that addressed this relatively new form of transnational crime. And having completed an investigation into what was considered Russian organized crime, I felt confident I could master the art of global investigations. I soon learned that naivete was the great precursor to knowledge.

As I became increasingly fluent in the language and operations of transnational crime, I began to travel worldwide. No country was off-limits. Every country has a new and different dynamic or vibe. Italy, with its cultural affinity with criminal organizations, was different from Spain, which was the playground for the villains of England.

France and Germany were much more insular, and their criminal organizations were much more political and extremist.

The Caribbean islands were (under)worlds unto themselves, especially Antigua and the British Virgin Islands (BVI). And the Pacific Rim, China, and Japan were unlike anything I encountered in the West, except for Australia, which suffered from home-grown corruption and European and American organized crime groups. The common denominator, nonetheless, was the "honey trap."

Meeting with a rather attractive Chinese woman I had retained as an interpreter in Bejing, I was warned that efforts would be made to compromise me or, even worse, frame me for a crime I did not commit. As I was about to depart my hotel room, I heard a knock on the door. There she was. Looking quite seductive, she meandered over to my bed. I realized this would not end well if I didn't resist her obvious overtures. She started crying and asking me to "take me to America . . . or arrange for me to go there." Fearing I was set up, I immediately escorted her out of my room, realizing that what we spoke about had been intercepted and recorded. It proved prescient; years later, I would read about American businessmen being unlawfully detained for crimes they did not commit.

Absorbing all this information and translating it into operational knowledge provided me with a veneer of credibility. Not until I met, dined, and drank with those who lived in this dark and opaque world did I realize the extent to which the rules that governed investigating the Mafia in the states were null and void.

I was fortunate in one respect, however. I met Palmisano, who had retired from the CIA. He had started a global investigative agency with which I became affiliated for a short time. Palmisano was stationed in the former Soviet Union. He was running a bank used to launder money on behalf of the so-called "criminal class." Palmisano and I would often meet and discuss the movement of assets and funds from the illicit sector to the licit economy. It was an education few would receive in college, for it involved as much illegal chicanery by the CIA as by those disposing of their ill-gotten assets.

Some thirty years later, we witness a massive seizure of assets—real estate, yachts, bank accounts, art, cars—by Western governments due to the war engineered by the world's richest and most dangerous and evil oligarch. Vladimir Putin accomplished what all the Congressional hearings, provocations, and goading did not.

Asset forfeitures have become the weapon of choice in repelling an army of 150,000 conscripts as they savagely plunder a sovereign nation. An estimated $213 billion of Russian wealth—hijacked from the Russian people—is stashed in off-shore accounts of the rich and infamous.

Hopefully, this story will convince you that life does imitate art.

THE LAW IS THE DARK SIDE
OF JUSTICE

Nothing could have prepared me for what I would encounter as I entered the murky world of Russian oligarchs. Who would have anticipated corralling one of the most prolific money launderers as a client and descending into the darkest corners of the Kremlin's opaque money machine?

Vladimir Berman, who lived in New York City and Los Angeles, California, had contacted me through a mutual acquaintance, Victor. I had known Victor for many years and used his knowledge to investigate organized crime in the New York metropolitan area. Victor was a Russian Jew who lived in Brighton Beach, New York—commonly referred to as "Little Odessa" or "Odessa By The Sea."

An enclave of Russian emigres was attracted to its waterfront, reminding them of Odesa, which was part of the Soviet Union. You could walk the boardwalk any day and see hundreds of men, women, and children frolicking on the beach or huddling under blankets on the benches that populated this seaside playground.

And a playground is what it was and still is. In the evenings, "Little Odessa" became an adult playground with neon signs promoting restaurants and nightclubs. The only way to enjoy this hedonistic Disneyland for the uninitiated is to go there with Russians who are "connected."

Not "connected" in the sense that suggests being a "made member" of the Mafia. Instead, someone like Victor, who knew the so-called "good guys," the "wannabe's," and of course the "bad guys," most of whom had partnerships with the restaurant and nightclub owners or their custodians.

"Odessa by the Sea" is everything featured in the 1994 movie *Little Odessa,* starring Vanessa Redgrave and Tim Roth. Women dressed in sparkling and bright-colored gowns, with flashy jewelry, prancing with their *married gatsby.* It is where every Soviet-era émigré who set foot on this "Shangri la by the sea" could realize the American dream. If you can make it here, you can make it anywhere.

But organized crime is woven through virtually every aspect of life in "Little Odessa." Restaurants, nightclubs, and strip joints are nominal fronts for human traffickers, drug dealers, extortionists, arsonists, and killers, some of whom came from the shores of Ukraine's Odesa. Contract killings were a way of life in "Little Odessa" during the '90s. The National and the Metropole were the go-to nightclubs where being seen added to your cachet. Here, the Russian mobsters and oligarchs would stroll in, usually dressed in black, and order bottles of *Jewel* and *Beluga* caviar. Money was no object, but credit cards were forbidden. Victor and I would go there several times, but it was apparent I didn't fit in. I stuck out like a sore thumb.

Time, of course, is the great equalizer. Being seen with Victor was an asset, but nothing was better than having a good-looking Ukrainian woman accompany me. I was divorced at the time and was dating a gorgeous divorcee who had emigrated from the former Soviet Union, now Ukraine.

Dasha was stunning, positively kryptonite. A head-turner, I would walk into the National or the Metropole, and the men would stare, and the women would seeth. Of course, to this day, I'm not sure who was more enthralled with this scene, Dasha or me. I suspect Dasha saw this as her opportunity to meet a wealthy Russian oligarch.

Recognizing and understanding the unspoken language is part of ingratiating yourself into a foreign culture. In "Little Odessa," I was in their world. They were not in mine. I either adapted like a chameleon or could be banished figuratively and, perhaps, literally.

One evening, Dasha and I decided to spend the weekend in "Little Odessa," soaking up the culture. Dasha could speak fluent Russian, which made me feel more comfortable. At least I would know when the punch or the bullet was coming my way.

Sitting in the National, we had a table to ourselves. Most everyone was with another couple or had a party of six or eight. While suggesting that Russians loved their vodka may be a stereotype, it was evident that night. Vodka and champagne were flowing quite generously.

Suddenly, one Russian man jumped out of his seat and started punching another Russian male. Before long, they were wrestling on the floor. People were screaming, and some were cheering, and the "bouncers"—three huge Russians—separated the parties. They returned to their table within minutes, enjoying the music and vodka. It was as if nothing had happened.

Of course, not every dispute resulted in a pleasant outcome. The National and the Metropole were known to have several murders, usually outside. Most were of competing criminal groups attempting to stake out their territory and a piece of the lucrative underworld rackets—human trafficking, prostitution, loansharking, gambling, and various white-collar crimes, particularly healthcare and stock frauds.

In retrospect, ignorance was bliss. I had no idea what lay ahead. This was the real deal, different from my years investigating the Mafia. The Mafia understood the rules here in America. The Russian mobsters could care less about rules. They had no qualms about eliminating family members, especially if they invited your family into their home. You were then the "gold standard"—accepted as one of them. Violate their loyalty, and the consequences could be pretty unforgiving.

Nonetheless, with Victor taking the lead, I became more familiar with the environment. Say little, look sartorially appealing (i.e., dress in black), drive the appropriate car (i.e., Mercedes), and listen and watch people.

People-watching became a passion of mine. Both intuitively and learned, reactions can say much about whom you are dealing with. Who does the talking and who does the listening can tell you about hierarchy? Who departs first and who leaves last are indications of respect. The women's reaction around the table to what is said can often reflect a particular disdain for the person or even admiration. Nothing can be more telling than the women's demeanor. Emotions say it all—sexism, in this instance, be damned.

Over time, Victor and I bonded to the point that we would visit one another, share family anecdotes, attend family functions, and generally stay in touch.

One day, Victor asked if we could go to Philadelphia to see the Liberty Bell, Constitution Hall, and the cradle of democracy. While driving there, Victor began sharing his life as a Russian oligarch, how he made his money, the government officials he had to bribe, and how he loved living in America. As we were talking, he mentioned how he had lost one million dollars in a real estate deal.

"How much," I asked.

"About a million dollars," he responded.

I almost stopped the car. I said, "You're kidding me . . . and you're not angry . . . I'd be livid. . . ."

"Why?" Victor said, "Anger will not get my money back; you will. . . ."

Realizing that Victor was sizing me up over the last year, I responded, "You must be kidding . . . and how do you expect me to do that?"

Victor quite calmly replied, "Let's talk another time . . . I want to enjoy what you call the cradle of democracy." Said, of course, in a somewhat sarcastic manner.

We both indulged in the historical artifacts that defined our democratic heritage. He did not realize that Philadelphia was once the capital of the United States. He found standing in Constitution Hall electrifying in that he believed the success of the industrial revolution in America was wedded to the rule of law. He would say, "at least here in America, you have a system that makes business agreements enforceable . . . I have to bribe to enforce business agreements."

Of course, I would say sarcastically, "well, so do we . . . it's called a legal retainer and quite costly legal fees. . . ."

He and I would laugh, both acknowledging that words have consequences.

As the day wore on, Victor suggested we have dinner. There was an iconic restaurant on the Delaware River, Moshula, with a rich and storied history that I knew he would enjoy discussing over dinner. And it was featured in *The Godfather*—another piece of Mafia symbolism.

I could feel that Victor's attention span was waning. He had more on his mind and did not want to engage any longer in history lessons.

"Marty, I want to discuss how you will get my money back . . . I trust you have people who can make things happen. . . ."

I just sat and listened while sipping on a nice glass of Amarone.

"Marty, now listen carefully," he said. "I gave a friend In Colorado one million dollars in cash to buy me a home in Aspen, Colorado . . . He told me the deal fell through . . . the builder stole my money . . . and he is trying to get it back, but he needed time. . . ."

I was floored. One million dollars in cash. My first question was, "do you have the contract you signed with him?"

Victor's response was simply a grin, like, are you serious? "There was no contract . . . This was a friend we vacationed with, invited into my home; our children knew one another . . . He was more than a friend; he was family. . . ."

"Well, you must have a check or an electronic transfer receipt?" I countered. Again he gave me a sly smirk. In other words, no.

Naturally, I lectured him about family and friends and how those you trust the most are the ones who will likely steal from you. "So Victor, you trust me . . . and now I will steal from you . . . this will not be cheap nor easy . . . you have no legal contract . . . you have no financial receipts indicating you gave him a million dollars . . . it was all word of mouth . . . he lives in Colorado . . . he is an American citizen . . . you live in New York . . . you are a Russian. . . . the optics are terrible, never mind the legal issues which may be irresolvable . . . Victor, you're fucked . . . how could you give a stranger one million dollars in cash . . . ?"

Non-pulsed, he responded, "first, he was a friend, not a stranger . . . and when you make ten million dollars a year, a million is not that much. . . ."

I almost dropped. The point was well taken. Everything is relative.

Little did I realize that this was, you guessed it, laundered money. Victor was washing his money through high-end real estate in Aspen—the playground for the rich, famous, and infamous. As I had finished the remaining bottle of Amarone, the wheels began to turn. How would I investigate the theft of one million dollars in Colorado, allegedly given by a Russian émigré? Not even David Copperfield could make his investment whole.

"Victor, let's keep drinking . . . I have to get pickled to figure out an investigative strategy on this one . . . and by the way, we're staying overnight in Philadelphia . . . I'm too drunk and tired to drive back to New York. . . ."

"No problem . . . where?" Victor inquired.

"I'll get us two rooms at the Fairmont, Victor."

Victor asked, "How much for the night?"

I was dumbfounded. He lost one million dollars and is concerned about the cost of a hotel room. "Victor, you must be kidding . . . you concerned about how much this will cost?"

Victor then told me this little anecdote that stuck with me forever. "Marty, this elderly man went into the hotel and asked the innkeeper for the least expensive room in the inn . . . The innkeeper was astonished. 'Why would you want the least expensive room in the inn? When your son comes here, he always stays in the most expensive suite in the inn.' The elderly man responded, 'that's why his father is a millionaire.'"

Of course, we laughed, and I told Victor I would book him into Motel 8, but I am staying at the Fairmont. He agreed and stayed at the Fairmont as well. His investigator wasn't going to live any better than him.

The following day, we departed Philadelphia for New York. Before leaving, I contacted a "connected" attorney friend, Sal Persico. Sal was not only "connected" to the traditional Mafia in New York but had family members involved in the fuel tax scam, which was the signature fraud of Russian gangsters. Sal suggested I drop Victor off in New York and then come to his office to discuss the matter.

At this point, I could see that I was slowly moving to the dark side. "Cash, a million dollars, no contract, no receipts, 10 million a year in income. . . ." This was big. At least, that's what I thought.

Little did I know that this was a paltry sum of money. Indeed, what lye ahead would ultimately become one of the biggest money-laundering scandals to hit the media waves. Vladimir Berman was sitting on the horizon, unbeknownst to me.

SLIDING DOWN THAT
SLIPPERY SLOPE

Meeting with Sal was always a pleasure. He would have the finest cognac and Cuban cigars in his office and was not stingy in sharing with me. Sal represented many mobsters and "made men," but he refused to socialize with them at family affairs. Sal believed that even the lowest criminal deserved a defense. He would, however, refuse to represent pedophiles, child molesters, or human traffickers—the latter engaging in acts of sadistic proportions.

Dispensing with the routine pleasantries, Sal asked, "Ok, Marty, what's up?"

"Sal, I have this Russian client who's been defrauded of one million dollars . . . but the problem is it was all in cash, and there is no contract or agreement, no financial documents, just word of mouth and a handshake. . . ."

Sal laughed. "Marty, he wasn't defrauded . . . his money was lost in the washing machine. . . ."

We both laughed. Of course, Victor was laundering his money with the crook who stole it. Some would call it poetic justice.

"So Marty, what do you suggest we do?"

I had been thinking about this all night.

"We need to confirm that Mr. Colorado (for want of a better name) had taken the money, Sal." The only way we could confirm this arrangement was with a conversation. Victor had to either record Mr. Colorado admitting to it over the phone or meet with him and "wear a wire."

Sal agreed. "Run this past your client, and let's see if he bites," he responded.

Victor and I met for dinner later in the evening. I suggested we meet at the renowned Sardi's in mid-town Manhattan, adding to the optics. I found it the perfect metaphoric atmosphere for planning an investigative strategy. Theatre is what I was about to engage in with Victor.

"Victor, I am going to make this simple . . . There is only one way I can proceed with this . . . I need Mr. Colorado to admit on tape, a wire, that he stole your money . . . without an admission, we have your word against his, and the courtroom is not your friend . . . Are you willing to record him or wear a wire?" Victor thought for several minutes and said yes.

Victor remained in touch with Mr. Colorado, abiding by the Mafia's adage, "keep your friends close and your enemies closer." He could call Mr. Colorado and arrange a meeting. He felt that Mr. Colorado would avoid talking on the phone.

We settled on this approach, and again, I finished the Amarone. With Victor, I drank and ate well. We departed with the ball in Victor's court. He would arrange a meeting with Mr. Colorado.

Several weeks went by, and Victor called me. "Marty, I can meet with (Mr. Colorado) in London . . . does that work?"

"No problem, Victor, but I have to get you the recording equipment and rehearse your lines."

We met later in the week. I provided Victor with a recording device and demonstrated how it worked.

I drafted a script that read, "Mr. Colorado, how will we resolve this situation . . . I gave you one million dollars in cash, and you're telling me that the builder walked away with it . . . I find that hard to believe . . . what happened?"

I said, "Victor, Mr. Colorado will likely stay with that story, which is fine. At least we will get an admission that you gave him one million dollars and the implication that it was for building a house . . . That's what we need, but if you can get him to say more and continue incriminating himself, that's icing on the cake. . . ."

Victor was psyched.

About two weeks passed, and Victor called me. "I'm meeting him in London on July 14th (1996)."

"Great," I said. "Now stay with the script and don't mess up with the Nagra . . . we need it recorded . . . your word means nothing . . . So much for the Constitution, Victor. . . ."

Sure enough. Victor flew to London, met with Mr. Colorado, and taped the conversation. We agreed to meet at the Tribeca Grill in lower Manhattan—again, the perfect metaphoric atmosphere. Bobby DeNiro, who played in *The Godfather*, owned it. The ambiance was perfect for a classic "sit down."

When I listened to the tape with Victor, he just grinned. He captured more than enough of the elements to pursue a legal case.

There was, of course, a fly in the ointment. Victor could not testify in a court of law. He would be eviscerated on cross-examination by a first-year law student. "One million dollars in cash . . . and where did you get one million dollars . . . a Russian émigré . . . ?" The optics would be terrible. So much for the rule of law, Victor! The "Gods of Guilt," a jury, would unlikely find in Victor's favor.

Entering the so-called "deep state" can be both challenging and exciting. You blindly poke around until you find the sweet spot. Mr. Colorado had a tax problem in Colorado, which would cause him more issues than this case was worth. It was our ace in the hole.

I brought the tape to Sal's office. We played it again. Sal was sold on the case and agreed to represent Victor.

I called Victor and scheduled a meeting with Sal. Meeting Sal in his office, he broke out the cognac and cigars. Being a bit of a physical fitness buff, Victor was reluctant to smoke a cigar with us. Cognac was a different story. After several cognacs, Victor puffed away as we planned our next step.

Now I had a Russian money launderer as a client.

A ROCKY MOUNTAIN HIGH

Colorado, here we come. It was the weekend of October 25, 1996. Victor had contacted Mr. Colorado and told him he would file a lawsuit for fraud and theft. Victor suggested that he get an attorney and have his attorney call Sal.

Mr. Colorado was rattled. Within a few days, Sal received a call from Mr. Colorado's attorney. Roger Rappaport was considered one of the premier attorneys in Denver. He had been on television several times. One trial on national television resulted in a not-guilty verdict for a bank robber caught on camera. Mr. Colorado was not taking any chances.

Sal was very cautious as to what he would share with Rappaport. He said, "I think it would be in your client's best interest for us to meet . . . we don't want this to spin out of control. . . ."

Rappaport got it. Monday, November 11, 1996, we would meet at 10 A.M. in Rappaport's luxurious office suite in Denver.

Sal and I left for Aspen on Friday, planning to enjoy the weekend in this most spectacular playground. We landed at Denver International and rented a car, which I insisted Sal drive. I had been to Colorado on several prior occasions, and the roads can be challenging—an understatement. No guardrails, steep embankments and cliffs, slick roads, and hairpin turns made this trip quite challenging, particularly given my aversion to heights. We stopped for a big juicy steak in Leadville en route to Aspen, but no Amarone. Roads were too treacherous to be drinking.

We arrived in Aspen, checked into the Big Nell, and relaxed in the hot tub before enjoying the village. Saturday and Sunday would be full days. Aspen proved the perfect getaway for what would be contentious negotiations on Monday.

Sal's connections were able to get us VIP treatment in Aspen. Through his New York "friends," we were "comped" with any wine we wanted—yes, Amarone.

Massages and entré to the most exclusive Club in Aspen—the Caribou Club—a members-only club. Sal, through his "friends," managed to get us admitted. There we met and drank with novelist and actress Roxanne Pulitzer, the former wife of Herbert Pulitzer, heir to Pulitzer Inc. The Club was crowded with many movie celebrities, literary mavens, and sports heavyweights. It was a fun-filled evening.

Sunday was our travel day. Again Sal commandeered our treacherous drive back to Denver. And again, we stopped in Leadville and indulged in another steak, but no Amarone.

We mosied back to Denver, checked into the Brown Derby Palace, rehearsed our proposal, and retired.

Monday morning, 10 A.M., we entered Rappaport's elegantly appointed office. If nothing else, the New York cache' provided credibility. Rappaport had a retired FBI agent who introduced himself to us in the office. At this point, we suspected an ambush. We were sure that Rappaport was aware of Victor's dicey situation and knew this would never see the inside of a courtroom.

Rappaport asked, "So what do you want?"

Sal confidently replied, "Victor's money . . . one million dollars your client stole from him."

Rappaport laughed and said, "so, where's the contract?"

Sal pulled out the recording, placed it on Rappaport's desk, and said, "play it."

Rappaport had this sophisticated surround-sound system, the phonics of which were incredible. He put the recording in the player, hit the play button, and listened as his client incriminated himself in a money-laundering scheme. Not only was Victor looking at jail, but so was Mr. Colorado.

After several minutes, Rappaport asked us to excuse ourselves. He called his client and discussed the dire implications of this dispute spinning out of control. He called us back into his office.

Rappaport asked us, "what will your client accept?" We ultimately settled on a 50-50 split. A half-million dollars were better than nothing. It was indeed a far cry from going to jail for money laundering.

Welcome, Victor, to the land of opportunity, where ju$tice is bargained, and bribes are costly negotiations.

RANDY FRANKLIN HIGH

AND THE BEAT GOES ON

Meeting with Vladimir Berman was a script out of Hollywood. Accompanied by a colleague from my office, we decided to meet at the iconic Plaza Hotel on the Upper East Side of New York City. Vladimir booked a room at the hotel and suggested we meet in what was then the famed Oak Room. Optics, particularly with Russian oligarchs, is critical to sending messages. Vladimir was setting the stage.

Arriving early, which allowed us to survey the environment, we entered the Oak Room, sat at a table, and our backs to the wall. This allowed us to see who entered the room and the patrons scattered throughout. We needed to understand the layout and the atmospheric vibe of the room.

Having never met Vladimir, I did not know what to expect. Nonetheless, it was not rocket science to know that this tall, slim, well-dressed man sporting an all-black outfit was Vladimir. He, of course, carried an Italian "carry-all" (i.e., purse). Accompanied by two heavier-set men, there was little doubt about who was in charge. Stereotyping be damned. The optics were compelling.

My colleague and I stood up and greeted Vladimir. He spoke fluent English but with a Russian accent. As I looked around the room, I saw several other people entering immediately after Vladimir. They were well dressed and may have been with Vladimir or tailing him. My antenna was laser-focused.

"Marty," Vladimir said, "You came highly recommended by Victor . . . He said I could trust you and that you treated him with respect."

Of course, I never thought of it that way. I merely treated him as another human being, no more nor less than I would treat any client.

Vladimir was telegraphing that he deserved respect as a Russian, notwithstanding the collapse of their economic and political systems.

Knowing what I had accomplished for Victor led me to believe that Vladimir had a similar problem. This was particularly troubling as I could sense I was sliding further down that slippery slope. I did not want to get involved in any more money laundering investigations. These investigations were quite dicey and were always gut-wrenching. And insinuating myself in this culture could prove quite problematic. Laws addressing money laundering and those involved could result in serious criminal charges.

Before speaking with Vladimir, I told him I wanted to go to his room—just he and I. "What for?" Vladimir ask.

"I'll tell you when we get to the room," to Vladimir's surprise. It was an unusual request and one that put Vladimir off balance. Nonetheless, he agreed.

Vladimir conferred with his colleagues, telling them in Russian that he was going to the room alone. Just he and I. My colleague stayed at the table where we were sitting. Vladimir's two henchmen sat at another table. Vladimir and I then departed to the elevator and went to the ninth floor, into his room.

Upon entering the room, I told Vladimir to strip down.

Vladimir looked a bit perplexed. "Why," he asked.

"I need to know that you are not recording our conversation," I responded.

"Why would I record our meeting? We have not even discussed why we are meeting," Vladimir opined.

I knew that, if nothing else, he would perceive my caution as a positive instead of insulting, even though he may have been offended. He agreed and stripped down to his underwear. Vladimir was clean. He dressed, and we proceeded to the Oak Room.

Returning to the table where my colleague had been waiting, Vladimir began discussing the specifics of our meeting. He was pursuing an investment opportunity with several individuals he claimed to know very little about. They were all Russian emigres. I found it odd that he did not have credible sources that could have provided him with the information. Nonetheless, his proposal intrigued me.

Moreover, he was willing to budget this inquiry quite generously. I listened intently and told him we would get back to him with a budget and a scope of services. He seemed satisfied; we shared a shot of vodka and left.

Driving back to our office, my colleague and I discussed the surreal atmosphere. It was like a movie with Vladimir out of central casting. As smooth and confident as Vladimir was, we questioned his real motive for seeking our investigative expertise. Indeed, he knew many more people in the Russian community than we did, some of which could alert him to any issues involving his potential partners. But we agreed that it was still worth pursuing. The assignment intrigued us, especially given the euphoria that had captured the Western world then.

Two weeks later, I contacted Vladimir and arranged for a second meeting. This time, Vladimir suggested Atlantic City at the Taj Mahal Casino-Hotel. That was doable, and my colleague and I agreed to meet him there.

Upon arriving at the Taj, I called Vladimir, who was in his room. He invited us to his room, an opulent suite overlooking the Atlantic Ocean. He had some better spirits and more refined wines but no Amarone. He had a superb Napa Valley Cabernet from Chateau Montelena. We opened the bottle and began drinking. Vladimir had one glass and then switched to a cognac. My colleague and I finished off the Cabernet.

We presented Vladimir with our proposal and the costs associated with the due diligence. We came in extremely high, thinking that Vladimir would negotiate downward. He didn't blink an eye.

When can you start," Vladimir asked.

We said immediately.

Vladimir then went to his finely handcrafted leather briefcase and pulled out a sheaf of papers. Each page had a name, address, prospective age, or date of birth. Vladimir wanted as much information on each person, five in all, as we could uncover. Time was of the essence; the sooner, the better.

An assignment of this nature, especially before universal access to the internet and worldwide computer databases, would encompass inquiries from sources in the law enforcement community, foreign services, and the Russian émigré community.

He was adamant that these inquiries were to be discrete—not overly intrusive. Leveraging a network of current and former Central Intelligence assets, FBI resources, and state law enforcement agencies, we felt relatively confident that we could deliver. We continued to question Vladimir's real motive behind this assignment. Something much more sinister was at play.

Over several decades, I developed a fairly extensive network in the intelligence and law enforcement communities. In addition, a robust "gray market" of private entrepreneurs could capture data and information from various sources (i.e., banks, telephone records, lodging receipts, stocks, etc.). With the budget provided, and given that the costs of this information were a line item that would be above and beyond our budget, we felt comfortable that we could deliver a cost-sensitive and credible product.

Notwithstanding our overly-optimistic perspective, as the assignment progressed, it became apparent that the initial retainer of $15,000 would be too little. We doubled our initial retainer.

Again, Vladimir didn't blink an eye. There were to be no fingerprints on these inquiries. Naturally, we could understand Vladimir's concerns. He wanted to remain as distant from this assignment as possible. The reasons became even more evident as we began our inquiry.

Vladimir gave us the names of several people. Naturally, we became increasingly suspicious of Vladimir's motive(s). Only cash was undoubtedly a major red flag. Indeed, Vladimir's money was more than likely "dirty." Meeting at the Taj Mahal, a casino, raised another red flag. Casinos were a vehicle to launder money, and as we learned years later, the Taj Mahal was a conduit for laundered cash from Russian oligarchs.

Our first inquiry was, you guessed it, Vladimir Berman. Who was he, and what was his pedigree? The results were eye-opening and bone-chilling.

Vladimir was a 32-year-old Russian émigré from Riga, Latvia. He was a computer genius in the software business for several years. He partnered with Mikhail Fedorov, a former KGB member. Fedorov served as a KGB agent in Africa with Boris Rosenstein, who eventually moved to Moscow and engaged in foreign currency trading. Vladimir and

Rosenstein would exchange rubles for hard foreign currency. They created fraudulent portfolios and borrowed monies from the IMF and other international lending institutions. They had no intent on repaying these loans. They would deposit the funds in Swiss bank accounts.

The accounts were registered to various shell corporations to which Vladimir had exclusive access. Ultimately, Vladimir acquired a vast amount of money, allowing him to open banks in Riga, Latvia, and Moscow, Russia. From Russia, Vladimir opened branches in Ukraine and Kyrgyzstan. He assisted Alexander Lukashenko in establishing a national bank in Belarus.

What better way to launder money than through your bank? We had seemingly stumbled onto an oligarch on law enforcement's radar.

As we continued to dig further, we uncovered Vladimir's significant real estate investment in Temecula, California, an upcoming wine destination. There Vladimir ensconced himself in the local culture.

Joining one of Bulgaria's more notorious crime figures, Peter Ivanov, Vladimir opened up an investment fund, Veritas Investments. Ultimately Vladimir had finagled himself as a director on the board of a prominent bank in Los Angeles, West Coast Import Bank and Trust.

His partner Ivanov died under mysterious circumstances in a vehicular accident in Bulgaria.

Vladimir had banks in Riga and Moscow, shell corporations in Switzerland, and Naura, an investment fund in the United States. He was a director of a prominent bank in Los Angeles. The stage was set to service clients from the former Soviet Union, dumping billions of cash into the American economy.

Naturally, our inquiries into Vladimir had alerted the antennae of the respective sources in our network. Our client Vladimir had paid us to develop profiles on several individuals. And here it was, our client, who appeared to be at the top of the totem pole. Nonetheless, we soldiered on, developing portfolios on Vladimir's list of people.

Unless you enter this shady world of corporate investigations, you are at a loss in understanding the nuances and competing interests often at play. You are searching for information that can *compromise* your client's adversary and benefit your client.

It may simply be personal indiscretions that reflect on the adversary's character. It may be legal problems like the litigants' nasty allegations during divorce or inheritance filings.

A whistleblower or disgruntled employee who feels that s/he was unfairly punished can be a valuable source.

And it may be a serious issue, such as insider trading, theft of monies, embezzlement, extortion, and physical harm.

Let's face it, only those with a problem or issue seek the services of a private investigator. It's essentially what the business is all about.

Vladimir searched for any information that would give him pause to engage in a business venture with the people he provided. Or at least that is what we believed when we undertook the assignment.

Although we were uncomfortable working for Vladimir, we understood the nature of the business. Persons with lily-white characters seldom retain you.

Almost every client had a tawdry history. Vladimir was no worse than most clients, many charged with horrendous crimes or civil violations. There were no indications that he was engaged in criminal activity.

Transactions in cash are not in and of themselves illegal. *Pecunia non olet* (i.e., money doesn't stink). We felt that as a wealthy Russian Jew, he was unfairly stereotyped. Or at least that's how we rationalized our engagement.

Relationships with the KGB were not dispositive of any nefarious activity, no more than my relationship with the CIA. Naturally, we had to be concerned that we were not involved in government-sponsored investigations that might compromise us and violate laws that would have made us agents of a foreign government. We were treading on relatively new and virgin territory.

We decided to move forward with the due diligence cautiously. We understood this assignment, and others that might follow said as much about who we are as it did about our client. But you learn from others. In this world of transnational money laundering, who would be a better teacher than someone who perfected the skill?

The following person we would put under a microscope was Gennady Molchalin. Gennady was the Director of the Russian Income Bank bank in Moscow. During his tenure with the bank, Molchalin was involved in the embezzlement of several million dollars earmarked for the military. When he learned of the investigation, he destroyed all the bank records. He fled to the United States to avoid charges and resided in New York City. Molchalin invested in several restaurants and a Brighton Beach, New York nightclub. He was considered a very close friend of an infamous Russian mob boss.

Next in our sights was Boris Rogov. Boris was an electrical engineer who worked on nuclear submarines in Russia. He also served in the KGB, stationed in Riga, Latvia. He ultimately immigrated to the United States and lived in Austin, Texas. We were unable to develop any compromising information on Boris.

Vladimir Krupin was interesting because he was a partner of Berman in Latvia and now lived in Temecula. It was rather unusual for Vladimir to have requested due diligence on Krupin unless there was another motive.

We suspected Berman was using us to uncover what information may have been available to law enforcement on the persons he had and was involved in business arrangements. It was a classic counterintelligence operation. Again, we questioned whether we wished to go any further and complete the assignment.

We decided to investigate the remaining characters and determine our course of action.

Fortunately, we struck the "mother load."

Yuri Golubev, the director of the leading helicopter manufacturer in Ukraine, had taken out over $100 million in loans from the Russian Income Bank in Moscow. In the same bank that Molchalin was a Director. Then Golubev relocated to New York and insinuated himself in the investment banking community. The loans defaulted.

As luck would have, we were able to contact one of the premier investigators of the Russian mob, who had recently retired from the New York City Police Department. Michael Savage was the savviest and most knowledgeable investigator who understood who's who in Brighton Beach.

He knew of Golubev and his associates. Repeatedly, he warned us that we were "reaching into the inner bowels of Russian organized crime . . .

These are dangerous people . . . you wanna tread carefully . . . they are not like anything you investigated before. . . . they kill and make it look like suicide. . . ." Savage opined.

Referring to an old Russian proverb, "the less you know, the longer you live," Savage suggested we may wish to reconsider the engagement.

Warning well taken. Nonetheless, we felt immune from retribution so long as Berman was our client (i.e., roof). But would he be when things got dicey? Remember, no fingerprints. Berman would likely disavow any knowledge of us or who we were investigating.

By now, this investigation's momentum was getting away from us. Journalists had uncovered what they believed to be a massive money-laundering scheme involving Russian emigres and one of the most prominent banks in New York.

Bankers United Trust was considered one of the top five banks in New York. It had assets of over two trillion dollars. Its Board of Directors comprised some of the country's most influential and wealthy business-people, political types included. This was huge, and its implications could make the banking industry shutter.

We now realized that we were in the vortex of a major scandal, the likes of which would send the stock of Bankers United Trust into the toilet. Never did we anticipate Berman would be implicated in this scheme.

The business of banks is the accumulation of money. Its origins are the business of law enforcement, not banks. Except for the fact that the government licenses and insures banks. Federal guidelines state, "Banks should take all reasonable steps to ensure that they do not knowingly or unwittingly assist in hiding or moving the proceeds of corruption."

With shell companies, however—companies that are paper only and shield actual ownership—and limited liability corporations (LLC), oligarchs, among many other persons, can legitimize their money pretty quickly. The beneficial owners are generally unknown, substituted by attorneys and accountants. There is no obligation to determine the source(s) of the monies. Banks are inoculated against any claims of "willful blindness." They are merely servicing a legitimately registered shell company instead of a named oligarch who may have made his money through illegal activity.

Indeed, the loopholes in the "know your customer" and "money laundering" laws are large enough to navigate an aircraft carrier. Again, *pecunia non olet* dictates.

More than 50% of the residential real estate valued at over five million dollars in the United States is purchased using shell companies. The buyers rarely acquire a mortgage, which could be dispositive evidence of ownership. Cash is the currency of choice. It is the bank's natural competitor.

The buyer's privacy (s) is the real estate broker's primary concern, not the cash source. And foreigners who are not United States citizens have a distinct advantage—they are not required to file an income tax return under most circumstances. Hence, this eliminates Al Capone's Achilles heel.

This led us to believe that Berman and his cadre of nefarious characters had merely exploited the loopholes in our financial system and avoided crossing the line.

Only time, of course, would determine if we were right.

THE LAUNDROMAT BECKONS

Sitting in my room at a hotel in Lake Como, Italy, I received a phone call from a reporter from the *Wall Street Journal*. How he found me in Italy is beyond me. Someone close to me gave him the hotel I was staying at.

"Mr. Grimes, this is Bob Aldrich of the *Wall Street Journal* . . . A mutual friend gave me your name . . . He suggested that I speak with you regarding a scheme at Bankers United Trust involving Russians and the laundering of money. . . ."

Naturally, I froze. There was no way that I wanted to embroil myself in this debacle. "Sorry, Mr. Aldrich, but I have nothing to say."

"Maybe if I mention several names, you might reconsider? Aldrich said. "Does the name Vladimir Berman ring a bell?"

I knew this would not end well.

"Again, Mr. Aldrich, I have no idea who you are speaking of, nor do I wish to continue the conversation."

I then hung up the phone and fretted about the implications of taking this assignment from Berman.

Although we did nothing illegal conducting this investigation, the stench of representing Berman's interests would not serve us well. Nor would any grand jury subpoenas. Moreover, Berman would not be happy seeing his name slammed all over the newspapers—which it eventually was. These would not be happy times.

Our investigation, of course, was suspended. We knew that any more poking around would only stir up a hornet's nest. And we were likely to be stung. Let's face it. We were smack in the middle of this scheme.

Although we had no idea what we stumbled on, we knew it would not end well.

Days on end, headlines read, Bankers United Trust, the subject of a Federal Probe, Key Executives of Bankers United Trust Implicated in a Money-Laundering Scheme, Russian Oligarchs and New York's Banking Elite under Investigation. The headlines were endless and relentless, as were the details in virtually every financial newspaper.

Fortune Magazine ran a headline, "Russia's Robber Barons Got Their Start in Business Running Rings Around a Lumbering State. Now This Handful of Powerful Men Is Creating a New Economic Order Out of The Post Soviet Chaos."

Princeton University Professor Stephen Cohen dubbed them a "semi-criminalized oligarch" that had made ordinary Russians "suffer unduly and unjustly."

"But as the banking elite extends its tentacles into Russia's economic infrastructure, more foreigners will wind up doing business with them," *Fortune Magazine* writer Craig Mellow opined.

After the Soviet Union's fall or implosion, there was a legitimate belief that integrating their financial assets with the Western world would advantage both countries.

The ultimate goal of the West was to create economic interdependence. In merging and blending Western assets and natural resources with Russia's, the West would have leverage over foreign policy interests and economic inroads into a fledging and untapped economy. Prominent Western oil companies foresaw "black gold" bolstering their bottom lines. In what is now naive thinking, it was considered the prescription for peace (i.e., peace dividend) on the European and North American continents.

Ironically, it made Western countries dependent on Russia's gas and oil. Uncoupling these financial arrangements could be pretty demanding.

The war over Ukraine has demonstrated that this strategy has had a somewhat convoluted and paradoxical effect. Designed to strangle Russia's economy if Russia refuses to withdraw from Ukraine, it has challenged long-term strategic relationships with allies—both in the United States and other Western and non-Western countries.

Using asset forfeiture and money-laundering laws implemented to address organized crime in the United States, transparency will likely shine an unwelcome light on Putin's kleptocracy—a kleptocracy run like *The Godfather*, according to Alexandra Tolstoy. She witnessed Putin's savage methods as an insider in Putin's murky world.

We encountered a name that initially didn't grab our attention during our due diligence. Robert Peterson was a director in a registered shell company, Miramax Industries, LLC. It had been registered in Nauru but was operating out of Connecticut. Although he was Russian, he had Anglicized his name. Perhaps that is what marginalized his involvement in our minds. Certainly, implicit bias was at play.

Peterson was married to a senior vice president at Bankers United Trust—Natasha Koslov, a Russian émigré.

As we explored the relationships further, we learned that Koslov had a prior relationship with Golubov, who was previously employed at the Russian Income Bank. The dots were connecting. Using his wife at Bankers United Trust, Peterson may be involved in some questionable activity.

The federal investigation into Berman was heating up. At this point, our primary source of information was prominent financial newspapers and magazines, all of which carried stories on what was then a major money-laundering scandal. All we could think of was how to extricate ourselves from this debacle.

Because we had sourced much of our information on Berman from former CIA and FBI agents, we anticipated they would contact us to discuss what was evolving. And they did. There was not much more we could add to what they had already told us, except one.

The connection between Robert Peterson, Natasha Koslov, and Yuri Golubov, who had now insinuated himself in Peterson's and Koslov's orbit, raised a red flag. This connection led us back to Berman and Golubov's $100 million looting of the Russian Income Bank. The circle was closing.

Several elements cross the line from legal to illegal for those unfamiliar with money laundering investigations.

The origins of the cash are central to a money-laundering investigation. Did the cash originate from a lawful source, or was it the product of illegality? Russia's tax fraud and customs violations were insufficient to apply U.S. money-laundering laws.

Moreover, were the deposits under $10,000 to obscure the actual sum of monies deposited? It's referred to as "layering." Deposits over $10,000 require the bank to submit a Suspicious Activity Report (SAR). Using what they call "smurfs" (i.e., couriers depositing cash in many banks), money launderers remain under the $10,000 threshold. This, too, is a red flag.

Did the bank confirm the depositor's identity? Knowing your customer is yet another requirement for deposits above $10,000.

Were shell companies being used to move the monies? If so, were there violations of United States laws?

And did the bank, if appropriate, notify law enforcement authorities or FINCEN, the regulatory juggernaut that may initiate an inquiry? These were questions we were not likely to get answered.

We saw no advantage in continuing our due diligence investigation for Berman. We knew he would be preoccupied with federal and state inquiries and wanted to distance ourselves from further involvement. I arranged a meeting with Berman to discuss our withdrawal from the matter. We met at the Plaza Hotel, in the Oak Room.

We were, of course, concerned whether or not Berman was a source for the FBI or the CIA and simultaneously conducting a counter-intelligence mission.

We learned that Berman sponsored a Congressional junket to Russia, introducing them to Vladimir Putin and other political figures in the Duma. Indeed, his academic portfolio, exceptional computer skills, entrepreneurial know-how, and personal fortune made him a worthy asset to the political world, both literally and figuratively.

This time. I did not ask Berman to go to his room and disrobe. It would be a waste of time, given that he expected me to make this request. If he were a source for the CIA or FBI, they would have been wise enough not to plant a listening device on him. If they secreted a "bug," it would be where we were sitting. Regardless, what we would discuss with Berman was guarded. We were there to suspend or terminate the assignment.

"Vladimir, given the current climate, many of our sources have dried up. They are unwilling to speak with us or convey any information that might aid you in addressing your concerns regarding your prospective partners . . . ", I stated.

"I can understand, but I was conducting my due diligence so that I did not get involved in any situation that might run afoul of the government," Vladimir responded.

"I think that horse left the barn, Vladimir . . . You have already been tarred and feathered. You should retain counsel . . . This is not going to disappear anytime soon," I told him.

Vladimir showed little interest in discussing what he had paid us. His primary concern was minimizing the reputational damage he was confronting. There was little we could do in the public relations arena. We suggested he might consider retaining a high-powered public relations firm to address what was likely to be a lengthy investigation.

We departed on amicable terms but left our contractual obligation open-ended. We suggested that Berman revisit the due diligence issues when things calmed down. We knew that we were unlikely to see him again.

Daily, stories were carried in newspapers and television addressing Russian emigres and money laundering. This latest signature crime branded Russian emigres who had unexplained cash. And Vladimir Berman was in the vortex of this media frenzy.

The Manhattan District Attorney's Office investigated the Bankers United Trust. The United States Attorney for the Southern District of New York was involved in an investigation into Miramax Industries, LLC. As in many investigations, the New York prosecutors were competing, neither sharing information.

As we sat back and watched the investigation unfold, Berman was skewered in the press. Alleged that he laundered over eight million dollars thru wire transfers from Miramax, a shell company when he was the head of private banking for West Coast Import Bank and Trust. There was little he could do to control the direction of the investigation.

The investigation in New York was intensifying. Miramax, led by Peterson, had laundered billions through Bankers United.

The investigation was, at this point, bicoastal- never a good sign for sharing information. Like most investigations that involve competing agencies, it was only a matter of time before more and more information would find its way into the obsessively Russian-phobic news media.

Journalists clamored for headlines reinforcing a narrative implicating Russians in massive amounts of resources being sucked out of the Russian economy and invested and deposited in safe financial havens.

United States real estate has always been a favorite parking lot for unexplained cash.

According to news reports, Berman also had a stake in another bank, Pacific Charter Bank in Nauru. Nauru's reputation for transparency was not pristine. It was regarded as a haven for stashing cash offshore.

Pacific Charter Bank shielded the origins of the money pumped through Bankers United and West Coast Import Bank and Trust.

Nauru's opacity provided registered shell companies with sovereign immunity. In other words, traipsing across the globe, criminal actors and their activity develop a qualified immunity from prosecution. Overlapping jurisdictions are ill-equipped to address multi-jurisdictional organized crimes.

With the investigation expanding to the Asian hemisphere, the tentacles of this giant octopus had developed in ways we would never have anticipated. It all began with a simple due diligence inquiry that morphed into an international scandal involving one of the most revered banking institutions in the world.

There was, of course, another aspect to our due diligence that ended up playing out a decade later.

Veritas Investments, out of Austin, Texas, became enveloped in a securities fraud investigation. And Berman was found civilly liable for defrauding the investors of over 300 million dollars.

Berman understood at an early age that in the world of high finance and political deception, one thing is for sure; the underworld and the upper world are indistinguishable. Neither could exist without the other. Both are inherent in the structural pillars of capitalism supported by a political system that rewards wealth with all the accouterments associated with privilege.

Never underestimate the power of the invisible hand. Organized crime and the organization of crime lubricate the clunky wheels of democracy and, inevitably, an existential threat to a free society. It's the ultimate puzzle.

Despite all the media frenzy and law enforcement investigations, Vladimir was never criminally charged with money laundering.

RED SQUARE, LENIN, AND THE KGB

Arriving in the early morning at Sheremetyevo International Airport in Moscow, I was greeted by two Russian men and two former KGB agents. With the demise of the Soviet Union in 1991, the KGB transformed into the Federal Security Service or FSB.

I was in Moscow and, subsequently, in Minsk on business and meeting with colleagues in the private investigations business.

Acquiring information from the former Soviet Union was based solely on personal relationships. Anything could be obtained, provided you were willing to pay. There were no agreed-upon costs. You negotiated a mutually-agreeable fee with your client. Formality be damned. It was a very fluid arrangement that made personal contacts imperative.

Being a bit jet-lagged from my overnight flight, we proceeded to an apartment in central Moscow. I showered and freshened up before departing on a whirlwind Red Square tour. Shots of vodka and a round of toasts began before our journey.

Valery and Andrei were former members of the organized crime police. Gregori and Boris were former KGB members. They couldn't have been more accommodating. Although I never knew how much English the others knew, Valery was the lone interpreter.

Our first stop was Lenin's tomb. Surrounded by a glass enclosure, Lenin lay in state as if he were a mannequin. Lenin was a hero to the Russian people. He was the forefather of the modern Russian state until Gorbachev eventually dismantled it. *Glasnost* and *perestroika* prevailed.

Among the older Russian people, Gorbachev was *persona-non-grata*. He destroyed the empire and embarrassed the Russian people, especially in the Western world. It was almost a replay of Germany post World War I.

While my hosts were embarking on a new experience after emerging from the remnants of communism, they did not want sympathy. They bravely confronted this new world and only wanted to be treated with respect.

This was certainly not an issue for me. I was aware of the scars of losing a war—Viet Nam. In their case, it was the Cold War. They now had to pick up the pieces and start over again.

Citing a favorite Russian proverb, "Do not criticize the mirror because you have a crooked nose," the West had no reason to presuppose moral superiority because the Russian economy was in shambles. Unfortunately, it had.

A day of sightseeing ended with a traditional dinner at one of the better Russian restaurants in Red Square. Having been accustomed to Russian culinary appetites, I learned that the richer the food, the better. All, of course, accompanied by rounds of vodka or Champagne. They certainly knew how to enjoy their newfound freedoms.

Over dinner, we discussed rebuilding an economy from the ruins of the communist ideology. Instead of arbitrarily-imposed quotas, market forces would dictate success or failure.

They questioned how the private investigative business operates in a market economy. They were interested in entering this field of endeavor, especially given the covert and investigative skills they learned in the KGB and the organized crime units of which Valery and Gregori were members.

"How do you find clients," Valery asked.

I explained to him that in this business, prospective clients find you.

"This is a word-of-mouth business . . . your reputation is your gold standard . . . never over-promise . . . it is better to level with your client from the beginning . . . they will likely be less disappointed if the results are not what they expected . . . you can always deliver more, but delivering fewer results is an unhappy client. . . ."

Boris was interested in how to cost an investigation. "How do you decide how much to charge a client," Boris asked.

"This is a very tricky and delicate topic . . . every client has a different pain threshold . . . when it begins to hurt financially, and they say ouch, you know to renegotiate your pricing . . . there is no definitive formula . . . you establish an hourly rate, estimate the amount of time the assignment will take, and keep the client continuously abreast . . . you should always get a retainer and have the client sign a retainer agreement . . . handshakes are not acceptable in this line of work . . . your client is not your friend . . . ", I responded.

This was a tutorial on the private investigation business. I had no problem educating them on the nuances. I was their guest, and my safety and security depended on them. In a communist country, you learn that your every move is scrutinized and tracked. You have little protection except for the goodwill of your hosts.

Andrei focused on how I acquired information, given the privacy issues constraining an investigation.

"In Russia, privacy doesn't exist . . . we can get anything on anybody . . . there are no rules that we must follow . . . we collect all kinds of information on people. . . . I can't understand how you can conduct investigations in the United States . . . , Andrei wondered?

I pointed out that prior law enforcement and foreign service relationships are critical in conducting investigations. Developing sources within the profession or social community of the person investigated can be invaluable. Legal documents filed by a litigant to a divorce, bankruptcy, or business or whistle-blower disputes can be a roadmap.

Legal depositions are another source of information, as are financial documents filed on behalf of corporations and partnerships.

Partnering with a law firm provided legal protections not available to a private investigator.

Indeed, discussing this through our interpreter, Valery, was exhausting for him and me. Nonetheless, it would open up the door for me the following day.

As the evening was winding down, we decided to begin the following day with a *banya*—our answer to a brisk massage. As I retired to my room, it was hard to fathom that I was among former KGB operatives in Moscow. It was, at that time, the nineties surreal.

Waking up the next day, my hosts greeted me. We had breakfast—coffee, bread, and eggs. We then departed for more sightseeing around Moscow and the *banya*.

Getting a Russian massage is undoubtedly different from anything I have ever experienced. First, you stripped down and sat around a table. On the table sat salted fish and vodka. You indulged yourself in the fish and imbibed in the vodka. This routine was the precursor to entering the sauna room, with temperatures exceeding 200 degrees Fahrenheit.

There were different levels or benches, each graduating to a higher temperature. At one point, Andrei challenged me to the highest level, more than 200 degrees Fahrenheit. I accepted the challenge, and after about three minutes, Andrei conceded. It was too excruciating for him. Jokingly, I said, "I guess American strength wins out over Russian knowledge," with us enjoying the kibitzing.

Sitting in this sweltering room, we were struck and stroked with white birch branches that drew welts on our skin. These welts extract toxins from the body, cleansing the immune system. Whether this was some legend, myth, or just plain quackery didn't matter. The experience was refreshing.

After sweating profusely in the sauna, we immersed ourselves in the ice-cold plunge pool. Refreshed, we gravitated to the table and continued drinking vodka and eating the salty fish. Now it was my turn to ask questions.

"Boris," I said, "is it true that the KGB embedded themselves in the Red Cross?" He laughed and said, "of course, so did the CIA and all the other intelligence agencies . . . what better beard is there than the Red Cross?"

Traveling in Communist countries, you learn that security services usually know your presence. Visas are required. Connections to the security services would be known to the authorities in the host country before you arrive. The same, I am sure, holds true here as well.

Spying is an inevitable consequence of both closed and open societies. It protects our freedoms and oppresses others, particularly in authoritarian regimes.

Echoing the renowned communist philosopher Karl Marx, "neither a nation nor a woman is forgiven for an unguarded hour in which the first adventurer who comes along can . . . possess them."

Assume every room you are in is "bugged." Don't be led into a sense of false security by putting the television or radio on; today's technology can factor the noise out.

Tourist agents are most likely KGB/FSB agents; assume they are fluent in English. The KGB/FSB routinely employs lip readers.

Someone who can deflect attention (i.e., a beard) is part of the intelligence services protocols when traveling in communist countries.

Although I never felt comfortable or safe, I was fortunate in Russia to have former KGB and organized crime investigators as my beards. Nonetheless, with the KGB/FSB, you never know who to trust.

As the day unraveled, we were to depart Moscow for Minsk, Belarus, at 9 P.M. The overnight train would arrive in Minsk in the early morning. We had two compartments with four beds. Boris would remain in Moscow, while Valery, Andrei, and Gregori would travel to Minsk.

Before we departed Moscow, Boris invited us to dinner at his home. There I met his family and children. The children looked at me as if I were an alien from another planet. This was the nineties. Few Americans were invited into the homes of Russians. I am sure they thought I was from the other Evil Empire.

Dinner was all that I expected. Pelmeni, olivieri salad, beef stroganoff, and Baklava for dessert. We sat around the table, with Valery interpreting. Boris's wife, Tanya, was interested in my family. "How old are your children," she asked. "I have three, two boys and a girl, 8, 10, and 12 years old," I responded. "Are you married?" "No, been divorced nine years," I said.

I was, of course, suspicious of all these personal questions, especially from the wife of a former KGB agent. Still imbued with a Cold War mentality, I was reluctant to share too much personal information. But neither did I wish to be perceived as impolite or rude.

Ultimately, I succumbed to many questions about my personal life and how I lived in America. Being invited into their home was considered an honor. The least I could do was allow them into my world.

Time was closing in on us. We had a 9 P.M. train to Minsk. Run the clock out, I thought.

Boris invited Valery, my interpreter, and me into another room as we finished dinner. He opened up a drawer in a closet. He showed me several weapons, revolvers, knives, and listening devices.

"Marty, these were my tools of the trade when I worked for the KGB . . . I keep them as souvenirs from my days as a spy . . . you have nothing to worry about when you are in our company. . . ."

I wasn't sure why Boris shared this with me. Was he trying to scare me or bragging about his days as a spy?

Later I learned that he was easing any fears I might have traveling the country with Valery, Gregori, and Andrei. They were well-prepared for the train ride to Minsk.

As dinner ended and we left. I thanked Tanya for her hospitality.

"You have a lovely family. Thank you for sharing them with me," I said to Tanya.

I gave each of the children a five-dollar bill and told them it was a souvenir from their father's American friend. I wanted the children to realize that enemies once can be friends later. Not all Americans were their enemy.

Off to the train we were.

THE MIDNIGHT EXPRESS
TO MINSK

The train ride from Moscow to Minsk is 9 hours. Andrei took care of the ticket—he flashed the credentials he retained upon retiring from the organized crime unit. Or perhaps he wasn't retired? Who knew, and who cared? All I knew was that I was in good hands.

We boarded the train and settled into two compartments. Both were sleepers, with two bunk beds in each. There was a dining car, where we retired after setting our luggage in the sleeping cars. Of course, we were to have several nightcaps before going to bed. A bottle of vodka sat on the table. We started imbibing. Fortunately, age was on my side. I could stay with them. A show of weakness would not bode well. I went shot for shot until we decided it was time for bed. We retired with a quarter of the bottle left. Gregori and Andrei brought the bottle to their sleeper. Valery and I retired in our sleeper.

Valery took a revolver from his jacket and placed it under his pillow as we undressed. I asked him, "Valery, is this a dangerous trip?" He laughed. "Marty, it's no different than any other trip. . . . always be prepared for the worst, but hope for the best. . . ." Point is well taken. It would be no different in the United States.

As I crawled under the sheets, I noticed Valery take his belt off and tie it around the compartment door and the door sash. I asked Valery, "Why are you doing that . . . isn't the lock sufficient?" Again, he laughed, saying, "You can never be too safe." Valery always had a sobering response to my alarming inquiries.

As we traveled through towns, I would awaken to the screeching brakes as they went from one train station to the next. It was certainly not a restful sleep, but it was safe. I could not have imagined making this trip by myself. All I could contemplate were the movies dramatizing the cruelty imposed on American spies when imprisoned by their Russian captors. The film *Midnight Express* reverberated in my brain.

Arriving at the Belorussky Station around 6 A.M., a driver and a black sedan greeted us. We loaded our luggage into the car's trunk and proceeded to an apartment in a huge tenement building. Only four people at a time could enter the elevator. It was an old building with no modern conveniences like the United States. Dingy, lights out, or unworkable; it was not what I expected. Spartan or rustic would be an understatement. It certainly did not compare to Boris's stately apartment in Moscow.

Greeted by members of the internal organized crime and security forces, it had all the optics of a scene out of *Tinker Taylor Soldier Spy* or *Bridge of Spies*. Again, it was an electrifying experience I never thought I would ever have imagined.

Except for Valery, no one spoke English, or at least that is what they led me to believe. Having just made this nine-hour trip, we were hungry and needed a shower and fresh clothes.

When I asked if I could freshen up before breakfast, they laughed. "Typical American," Valery translated, "not used to the unpleasantries of travel." Whatever that meant, I had no idea.

Valery showed me the shower, and I indulged myself in a shower with the pressure of a crinkled water hose. Again, it was certainly not the Ritz Carlton or Motel 8!

As I dressed and re-entered the larger dining area, my hosts had breakfast on the table—coffee, bread, and eggs. We all sat around, with Valery interpreting the questions they were all asking.

Their interest was in the private investigation business and how we could develop a global investigative enterprise to service the emerging industries of the former Soviet Union. Their primary focus was making money—U.S. dollars, not just rubles—.

Of course, my thoughts immediately regressed to my experience with Vladimir Berman. Moving money out of the former Soviet Union had become the clarion call of American law enforcement. The news media was laser-focused on this topic. I could see monumental problems that could be game-changing and possibly physically dangerous.

I also realized that this arrangement could be very lucrative. The money these Russian businessmen were willing to pay was enticing. This business did not attract those "on the side of the angels." You had to be ready to undertake risky investigations involving persons with disreputable backgrounds. There was little to worry about so long as I didn't cross the line.

Indeed, the private investigation business involves less-than-honorable clients who have gotten themselves in trouble. Here, we contemplated a service that kept these businessmen from getting into trouble. It was prevention instead of intervention—at least, that is how it always begins and how I envisioned it.

"The slippery slope" is just that—slippery. Good intentions morph into disreputable outcomes. What begins as a simple due diligence matter evolves into a legal debacle. Enablers—lawyers, accountants, brokers, bankers, investigators—start with honorable intentions and then are swept into irreversible skulduggery.

I could see that my hosts were quite psyched about creating this global investigative enterprise. I certainly did not wish to disappoint them.

"Andrei, how do you expect to get clients," I asked, with Valery interpreting.

"That should not be a problem . . . we have plenty of businessmen here and in Moscow that want to bring investment opportunities to American businessmen," he responded.

"But how can I assure American businessmen that they dealt with reputable business people in Russia or Belarus?"

"Let us take care of that . . . that's our end of the deal. . . ." Andrei stated through Valery, of course.

It's a given; knowing who to trust regarding the KGB is never easy. You have to assume their craft is deception and obfuscation.

Being in the business for a while, I knew it was not as simple as Andrei proposed. Just as my involvement with Berman and Igor turned out, there is always a fly in the ointment. Anytime money is involved; there are complications.

"Andrei, you know the number one cause of divorce," I asked. Andrei was perplexed. "What does this have to do with what we are proposing?"

"Andrei, everything . . . money is the number one cause of divorce . . . and with what you are proposing, there will be some dissatisfied clients . . . are you prepared for the consequences when the client refuses to pay?"

Andrei and the group laughed. Anyone in this business knows the term "sticker shock"; the invoice often leaves the client unhappy.

It was now time to do some sightseeing around Minsk. Having little knowledge of the history of Belarus, it was undoubtedly another adventure steeped in *The Great Patriotic War* atrocities.

Belarus was part of the Soviet Union. When Hitler invaded, Belarus lost a quarter of its population and "practically all of its intellectual elite." Over eighty percent of the towns and villages were destroyed. Referred to as "White Russia," Belarus borders Ukraine, Russia, Lithuania, and Latvia. Today it is run by the so-called "Last Dictator of Europe," Alexander Lukashenko. It is a mafia state.

Visiting Independence Square (an oxymoron) in the center of Minsk was the site of violent clashes with the police and demonstrations protesting the corrupt Lukashenko regime. Independence left Belarus with the rigged election of Lukashenko.

The Minsk Sea was a sight of unrivaled beauty in a land-locked country. Mountains surrounded what was essentially a reservoir. Valery was proud of this water mass, where he took his children fishing and boating.

Perhaps the most moving symbol of Belarus's sacrifices in World War II was The Unconquered Man: Haunting War Memorial.

Stone pillars represented three million civilians slaughtered by the Nazis. Entering this memorial is a colossal bronze statue of Joseph Kaminsky holding his son, who died in his arms. Kaminsky was the last survivor of this untold carnage.

I could only feel the terror ripple through my body as I stood among these stone tombstones. Every 30 seconds, bells would ring, symbolic of the houses burnt to the ground. Few people realize the sacrifices of the Belarusian people during World War II.

A day of sightseeing always seems to end with a retreat to the *banya*. Again we all stripped down, savored the salty fish with vodka chasers, entered the sweltering sauna, enjoyed the caressing of birch branches and leaves over our bodies, and ultimately took a dip in the ice-cold plunge pool. Nothing is more invigorating than this uniquely Russian massage.

That evening we had dinner at the home of Gregori. Met his lovely wife, Sasha, and she prepared a traditional Russian dinner; pierogi and fixings. A classic dessert, Baklava, followed it. Of course, finishing the evening with a bottle of vodka became a daily tradition.

Retiring to bed in Valery's home never looked so inviting. All I could do was think about being in the middle of nowhere, yearning to return to the civilized world I relished.

However, the next day, Valery planned a trip to his dacha in the country. I would meet with several former KGB operatives and Belarussian organized crime unit members. I could only contemplate their questions and their suggested proposals.

After spending this much time with my hosts, I realized I was only getting deeper into this murky world of money-laundering investigations. No laws in Belarus or Russia addressed this issue; even if there were, enforcement would be purely symbolic. I realized federal law enforcement in the states was laser-focused on this activity, especially involving Russians.

Again, Valery, interpreting for those who spoke no English, intended to address the issue of a global investigative enterprise that could benefit both Russian and American businesses. He impressed upon me how lucrative it could be. I knew that money was only one consideration. Legality was paramount in my mind. Valery and his colleagues had little appreciation for the legal nuances that could envelop them in criminality. Nor was I convinced that I would not be tainted or shrouded in illegality.

Scheduled to leave on the 10 P.M. train to Moscow, it was now 8 P.M., and we had to return to Minsk and get our luggage. I assumed Valery, Gregori, and Andrei were returning with me to Moscow.

They told me they would be remaining in Minsk and that I would be returning to Moscow alone. All I could think was my *beards* had disappeared on me—I was on my own in the middle of nowhere.

There is not much to see on the train between Minsk and Moscow at night. It is pretty barren, with several villages in between. I collected my luggage, and they drove me to the train station.

Awaiting the arrival of the train, Gregori approached me. He asked me in fluent English to take three thousand American dollars to his daughter in New York. He said his daughter would meet me at JFK Airport upon arrival. She would have a placard with my name on it.

What choice did I have at this point? My well-being depended on Gregori and his colleagues, who were to meet me at the Moscow train station.

I secreted the money in my pocket. As the train arrived at the station, Andrei walked me to my compartment. He then demonstrated how to take my belt, wrap it around the compartment door handle, and secure it to the door sash. I now knew that my protection was simply a belt—no gun, knife, KGB, or police officers.

I can still smell the toxic fumes the train spewed as it awaited its passengers to board. As Gregori implored, I settled into my compartment, wrapped my belt around the door handle, and tied it to the door sash. I was tired, my adrenalin pumping and all I could think of was returning to the United States.

Andrei, Gregori, and Valery waved goodbye as the train pulled from the station.

Off I was to Moscow.

THE GREAT TRAIN ROBBERY

Few things are more frightening than being in a foreign country, unable to communicate in the native language, dependent upon your instincts and resources, and having no recourse if confronted with an unexpected or dicey situation. Perhaps ignorance was bliss. I merely soldiered on, unaware of what would occur in a couple of hours. What choice did I have?

About three hours into the train ride and tucked in bed, I heard the train slow down and stop. I was under the impression that we were picking up new passengers at a train depot. I lay in bed, waiting for the train to proceed. But it never moved. Unaware of what was occurring, I just sat in my bed and listened. I could hear passengers yelling. I heard a lot of screaming, although I had no idea what was said. Doors on the compartments were battered. All I could think of was what Andrei said might happen. Maurading bandits held up the train.

This was out of a movie. What was the chance that the train I was on would be held-up by bandits, and my protection was hundreds of miles away in Minsk? This was terrifying.

Sitting in my compartment, I heard the bandits approaching my room. I could not afford to show weakness. As my former KGB protectors often say, "to look weak is to get beat," a phrase I took with a grain of salt. Now it was real.

Inching their way to my compartment, they started to pull on the door. Fortunately, I secured the door with my belt. They banged on it, yelling in Russian. I had no idea what they were saying. The thumping got louder and louder. I could envision being taken as a hostage, tortured, or killed.

Finally, I decided to revert to my ways when working on New York streets. Act completely crazed, willing to kill or maim anybody in my way.

At the top of my lungs, I shouted, "Come get me, you mother-fuckers . . . I'll shoot the first one that comes through that door . . . come on in, you mother-fuckers . . . come on. . . ."

Of course, I could only speak English. They probably could not understand a word I was saying. But the inflection and tone of my voice were seemingly threatening, if for nothing else. The thumping on the door stopped. Whether I scared the shit out of them or they went on to easier prey, to look strong was not wrong. The words of my KGB protectors proved prescient.

The train stayed put for hours. Ultimately it started rolling again. It wasn't until I arrived In Moscow that I learned what had occurred.

I was two hours late. Boris and one police agent greeted me upon my arrival. There was a beautiful female translator that accompanied them. Marisha was her name.

Marisha told me that a barricade had stopped the train on the tracks. The bandits entered the train and robbed the unsecured compartments.

She asked me whether I was robbed. I told her that I had secured the door as Andrei had suggested. She laughed and said, "Andrei is one of our best agents . . . you were lucky to have had him as your friend . . . they don't come much better. . . ."

We then entered a black limousine and proceeded to the hotel I would be staying. Boris arranged an early check-in. My luggage was carried to the room. We had breakfast in the hotel's restaurant. We discussed the remainder of the day. After breakfast, I went to my room to shower—something Boris felt was unnecessary.

Through Marisha, Boris said, "Marty, we are going to the *banya* later . . . no need to take a shower. . . ."

"Boris, I just need to freshen up . . . a nice hot shower will reinvigorate me. . . ." Boris was okay with that.

I wondered if Marisha would join us in the *banya*. Who would interpret? My hopes were dashed when Marisha told me she would leave us at the *banya* and meet us in a couple of hours.

I was now left to my own devices. However, we made it work; we conversed through hand signals, smiles, and laughter. After being treated to yet another round of birch brooms, fish, and vodka, we met with Marisha. She suggested we go shopping at some local, non-touristy stores.

Sounded good to me.

Marisha was quite attractive and, above all, she did not smoke—a deal-breaker. Boris, Andrei, Gregori, and Valery smoked incessantly.

Marisha would accompany me into the stores and translate with the storekeepers.

At one point, we went into a jewelry store. I could see that Marisha was fascinated by one particular watch. I asked her if she liked it. Marisha was relatively diminutive, not wanting to appear too anxious. She nodded yes.

I asked her, "how much does the jeweler want?"

She asked the jeweler. In U.S. dollars, $450. I could see that she was embarrassed to tell me.

"Marisha, how much," I asked.

"Too much," she responded.

I then told Marisha that it would likely be more than the watch if I had to hire a translator. "So Marisha, how much is the watch?

"Four hundred and fifty dollars," she responded.

"I'll take it." Quarreling over the price, at this point, served no purpose.

When I handed Marisha the watch, she started crying. She hugged me. She asks that I not tell Boris and keep it on my person until later that day.

"No problem, Marisha . . . Boris will never know. . . ."

Marisha was concerned that Boris would be envious. Or that Boris would demand the watch. Or at least that is what I thought at the time.

Indeed not an unwarranted fear in a country that was scraping by after the collapse of the communist state.

This was my last night in Russia, so we planned a dinner at a local, traditional Russian restaurant. I invited Boris and his wife, Tanya. Marisha, who was not married, would be my guest and translator.

WARNING: BEWARE OF THE HONEY TRAP

The famous English spy novelist John le' Carre often peppers his stories with the ultimate indiscretion that trips up most American businessmen: the honey trap. I was now with this attractive Russian lady who deftly plied my loyalty from Boris. The slippery slope was about to become even steeper and messier.

Over dinner, Marisha would interpret, making the evening seem like it would never end. We enjoyed one another's company. Other than interpreting, Marisha was quiet and avoided personal interaction with Boris or Tanya.

Tanya was primarily interested in learning about America, the family, and schooling. Her questions were often prefaced with what she had read in newspapers and books.

Boris and Tanya were naturally apprehensive about Russia transforming into a market economy. The quality of life guaranteed by the state was relegated to the dustbin of history. Individual initiative would replace it. I attempted to ease their fears.

"Capitalism is not the bogeyman it's made out to be," I impressed them. "It can liberate you, forcing you to expand your horizons . . . it can reach into your untapped reservoir of creativity that you never knew you had . . . it can lead you to invent more efficient ways of performing worn-out tasks . . . and it can reward you quite handsomely . . . ," the latter point being where this conversation was heading.

If for nothing, the stereotype of the American was all about money, comfort, and success. Indeed, what I was preaching was alien to their way of thinking. Nonetheless, we had a spirited but exhausting conversation.

We had one last toast to our future joint venture as dinner ended. It seemed as if this arrangement was a done deal, at least in my hosts' minds.

Boris and Tanya had to excuse themselves, for their children awaited their return home. Boris said he would collect me at 7 A.M. the following day and transport me to the airport.

I was now in a somewhat awkward situation. Marisha suggested we go to the bar and get a drink. I knew where this was leading but reluctantly agreed.

I gave Marisha the watch she asked me to hold for her. Now we were drinking quite generously. I had to be ready early the following day for my flight home. Marisha had no intention of leaving. The opportunity was enticing. I remembered "the weak get beat," a phrase Valery would routinely raise.

"Marisha," I said, "I must get packed and get some sleep . . . let me get you a taxi . . . we can't let this go any further . . . you were a great interpreter and host . . . you are always welcomed to my home in the United States . . . who knows, you may even be involved in our joint venture. . . ."

We hugged, and Marisha gave me an inviting kiss. I knew that this could be dangerous. I also knew that any romantic liaison could lead to unintended consequences. Deception is the craft of the KGB/FSB. For all I knew, Marisha may have been KGB/FSB. While we both were disappointed, "the weak get beat." Extricating myself from the situation was the most logical recourse.

Marisha got in the taxi, and I went to bed; opportunity dashed.

At precisely 7 A.M., Boris was there to collect me. And so was Marisha. I looked to see if Marisha was wearing the watch. She was not. Of course, I was concerned that Boris would discover I was part of Marisha's deception. I thought this may have been a test by Boris, obviously challenging my integrity.

At this point, there was no way of knowing. All I wanted to do was board the airplane and return to the United States.

Passing through immigration and customs, I was concerned that the money I carried on Gregori's behalf would be found and confiscated.

How would I explain this to Gregori? Would he believe me? Or would he think I stole the three thousand dollars? Again, that slippery slope was getting trickier.

It was the cost of doing business in Russia and with Russians. Deception and dissembling are a way of life. "Good lies are a gift," as Valery would say. "Just make sure they are good and you don't get caught." An ominous warning.

As the plane lifted off the runway and the landing gear retracted, I breathed a sigh of relief. I was headed back to New York to safety, familiarity, and family.

THE EYE IN THE SKY IS
NEVER FAR AWAY

While the degree of cyber spying in the 90s was not as sophisticated as today, make no mistake—it was every bit as pervasive and insidious. Not only were my meetings in Moscow and Minsk surveilled, my telephone calls and conversations monitored, and my hotel room bugged, but the CIA welcomed my return to the United States. Little did I know that when I departed the plane at JFK, a CIA agent would be there to greet me.

"Mr. Grimes, my name is Jack McComb. I want to speak with you."

"Who are you . . . I have no idea who you are . . . what do you want to talk about? . . ." I responded.

McComb said, "Can we go to the Port Authority police station?"

"Sure, but first I have to meet someone . . . can I meet you there?"

"I'd rather you come with me first . . . that's what this is about," McComb said.

I realized that the CIA had intercepted Gregori's conversations with his daughter. And, of course, my name was part of that conversation.

"No problem, let's go."

McComb was in a hurry. He knew the daughter might become suspicious if too much time had passed.

After showing me his credentials, he said, "so let me have the three thousand dollars you are carrying . . . I will give you three thousand dollars in new bills, which you can give to Gregori's daughter. . . ."

We exchanged the cash—$100 bills. I proceeded through immigration and customs. As I entered the main passenger terminal, I noticed a younger woman standing with a placard bearing Marty Grimes. It was Gregori's daughter. After a few pleasantries, I introduced myself to her and gave her the money. She thanked me, and we departed.

When I was confident that I was no longer in the daughter's sight, I returned to the Port Authority police station. Now for the messy part.

McComb was there to debrief me on my trip to Russia and Belarus.

"Who did I meet with . . . what did I learn . . . what arrangements were made for future meetings . . . how did I communicate with Gregori, Boris . . . with Valery . . . ?"

And, of course, with Marisha?

That he knew about Marisha naturally raised my antennae. "How do you know about Marisha?" I asked.

"That's my job," McComb responded.

Now I wanted some answers.

"Was Marisha KGB?" I asked.

"Would I be asking about her if she wasn't?" McComb sarcastically responded.

I knew the CIA had enough information about my travels to Russia and Belarus to cause me grief. It is better to cooperate than become confrontational. Additionally, my prior relationship with Palmisano would serve me well in building a rapport with McComb—or at least that's what I thought.

I suggested that we meet at another location the following week. McComb agreed. We agreed to meet at the offices of Sal Persico, my attorney-friend, the following Friday. We would meet at a location that benefited me rather than an office he would likely have wired.

I departed the airport and drove home. As I exited my car, I virtually kissed the ground. Being back in the United States was nirvana. Only when you leave and experience what it is like living under an authoritarian government can you realize and appreciate our freedoms.

As Friday approached, I could only imagine what the day would be like. I'm sure McComb saw me as a potential asset, all the pleasantries aside.

I contacted Persico and told him as much of the story as possible. I asked if we could use his office and if he would join us in the meeting. He agreed. I told him to introduce himself as my firm's corporate attorney. He was okay with that as well.

I knew that I had not violated any laws or that the CIA was not interested in domestic criminal prosecutions, so I was comfortable sharing everything I learned with McComb.

Friday would undoubtedly be an eventful day that would only escalate the rapidly descending slippery slope.

Naturally, I thought long and hard about Marisha. Did Marisha set me up with Boris? Were Andrei and Marisha connected? Was there closed-circuit surveillance in my hotel room (I assumed there was)? What may have been the outcome if I had taken Marisha to my room? Would she have claimed a sexual assault?

There were so many questions and so few answers. In this messy world of transnational crime, you can never know how far you will descend into the abyss.

LIFE IMITATES ART

If there are few things you learn in life, one is sure. We have minimal control over our destiny. Events, primarily unexpected, can and often do change the trajectory. It may be an illness, a death, a birth, or in my case, an unexpected meeting. Serendipity keeps life interesting.

Had I known in 1994 that I would be entering the world of international espionage and cross-jurisdictional crime, I am not sure I would have chosen this career path. As intriguing and exciting as it was, many sleepless nights, ethical dilemmas, and close calls came with it. As I have learned a decade later, with the poisoning of Alexander Litvinenko, the KGB/FSB takes no prisoners. Betray the KGB/FSB at your peril.

When I met Valery, I had no idea he was involved with the former KGB. Naivete perhaps was to my advantage? Should I accept his goodwill and friendship at face value?

Charming, educated, and culturally sophisticated, I saw Valery as another asset in a vast network of global resources. In this business of private investigations, there is no limit to the number of human assets you can accumulate.

Of course, after dealing with Berman and that debacle, I should have learned my lesson.

Here I was amid international espionage and still intrigued with trying to make sense of the depths I was willing to descend. Might I have a death wish? Or does playing on the margins of life inspire me? I thought, get out while you can before you lose your soul—a warning that echoed in my head.

Friday arrived. We were meeting at 11 A.M. I arrived at Sal's office at 10 A.M. Upon my arrival, Sal seemed anxious to grab my attention.

"Marty, let's talk first. I have a situation that needs my immediate attention."

"Marty, I have a billionaire client who lives in Turkey. He wishes to remain anonymous . . . he has a son, Turgay, who is in Prague at this moment . . . his son has been acting strangely, withdrawing large sums of money from his bank account. . . . and running up huge credit card purchases . . . would you be interested in looking into this discretely," Sal ask?

I said, "Sal, let's get through the meeting with McComb, and then I will discuss this matter."

McComb arrived precisely at 11 A.M. No other agents had accompanied him. I assumed that he was recording me. And I am sure he thought I was recording him. The dance would be well-choreographed on both our parts.

"Marty, let me be clear," McComb stated. "I have no interest in your private investigations, your clients, or anything to do with your business. . . . my only interest is to see if I can use you to acquire information on Boris, Gregori, and Marisha . . . They have been on our radar for the last two years . . . they are part of an international money laundering ring . . . art, and real estate here in the states . . . I am only interested in their relationships in Russia and Belarus . . . we know who they are dealing with in the states. . . ."

"McComb, let me be straightforward as well . . . I am not interested in being your asset and putting my life in jeopardy . . . My interest is strictly making money and expanding my business to the former Soviet Union . . . there is money to be made there . . . lots of money," I responded.

"Our goals do not differ . . . all I ask is that you continue your relationship with Gregori, Boris, and Marisha . . . build up trust with them . . . we want to understand how connected they are to the powers in Russia . . . ," McComb opined.

Where this would lead was above my pay grade. But at this point, I saw no serious downside. Having McComb as a roof was a benefit. At least I had another asset to tap.

McComb departed, giving me his personal phone number if I needed to reach him.

Sal was non-pulsed with the meeting. He felt it was your typical CIA recruitment pitch that would go nowhere. Sal was more intent on returning to his client's drama.

"So, Marty, what do you think . . . are you in?" Sal reiterated.

My mind was racing. I was in Prague before. Palmisano had arranged meetings with a private investigative agency and several business people on my last trip to Prague. I could leverage that relationship and enjoy all Prague had to offer simultaneously.

Then a thought entered my mind which would propel me into a world that foolishly created more unnecessary drama.

Perhaps I could arrange a meeting with Marisha in Prague—a relatively short flight from Moscow?

"Sal, this might work . . . let me see if I can rearrange the pieces. . . ."

I contacted McComb to tell him I was arranging a rendezvous with Marisha in Prague, the Czech Republic. It would be under the pretense that I had a business opportunity there. I would contact Marisha and ask her if she would like to meet in Prague.

McComb seemed amenable to this arrangement. He gave me the name and phone number of an embassy colleague he knew there. I could only assume that it was the CIA.

Before I could call Marisha, she reached out to me.

"Marty, I've been thinking about you since you left Moscow . . . Is there a chance you are returning shortly?"

The approach could not have been more timely.

"Marisha, I have to be in Prague next week . . . I have business for a couple of days, but later, you and I could spend some time sightseeing . . . Would you care to join me there?"

Marisha was excited. "Definitely. When do you want me to come? I can leave tomorrow. . . ."

I advised Marisha that it would be easier if she came towards the end of the following week.

"I need to spend time with my colleagues there . . . I don't need any distractions. . . . let's figure Thursday. . . ."

"I will be there with bells and whistles," Marisha said.

"Marisha, where did you hear the term "bells and whistles," I asked.

"Isn't that what you say in America," she retorted.

"Yes, but how did you know that term?"

"I read a lot of American literature. Did you forget I speak fluent English, and it always caught my fancy," Marisha said.

Again, "caught my fancy" was so American. Was Marisha trying to impress me with her knowledge of American idioms? Or was she telegraphing her cultural familiarity with America—a sign of a deliberately-focused education? Did Marisha want me to know that she was a former KGB? Or was she making foolish blunders?

There was no doubt that Marisha was surveilled, as were her phone calls. Was she sending me a message? Only by meeting her face to face might I know the answer.

The investigation on behalf of Sal's client would serve as the perfect cover. Marisha would be the least suspicious, and it would burnish my cachet among those in Russia. There would be no question about Marisha telling Boris and Andrei of her excursion to Prague.

I assumed KGB/FSB would surveil me throughout my trip to Prague. I needed to consider some diversionary tactics to avoid round-the-clock surveillance.

I departed JFK International on a Saturday night, landing at Prague Ruzyne International Airport on Sunday. That gave me time to check into the hotel, recover from being jet-lagged, and plot my itinerary for the week. I always liked to arrive a day or two early to avoid last-minute catastrophes.

Upon arriving in Prague, I contacted Marisha, letting her know I had landed safely. Again, she said she could come earlier than Thursday. For me, that would only be inconvenient. She understood that I was busy but suggested she could visit several museums while working.

"Thursday, it is," I firmly intoned.

I told Marisha to take a taxi to The Grand Hotel in Prague's old town. I would have the front desk give her a key to my room.

It was far from ideal; allowing Marisha access to my room was problematic. Moreover, Marisha now knew where I was staying and could appraise her KGB/FSB colleagues of my comings and goings.

Anything less than this arrangement, however, would jeopardize my cover. There were no safe alternatives—just risk mitigation.

I decided to book a room at a hotel several blocks away. I would use this room essentially as a "safe house." I would go there when I wasn't with the business associates or to address issues out of Marisha's earshot. A circuitous route would be the new norm from here on out.

Marisha arrived late Thursday afternoon. She checked into my room. When I returned to the hotel, I immediately went to my room. There was Marisha, emerging from the shower. Marisha looked as beautiful as ever—even more than I remembered her.

At this point, the issue of romantic entanglements was moot. It was inevitable. Although that slippery slope had now become irreversible, I had crossed the Rubicon. There was no turning back.

We spent the night together, ordering room service until the wee hours of the morning. Fortunately, I had a safe house to retire to throughout the day, allowing me time to recuperate, speak with Sal, and rearrange my schedule. The term multitasking took on a whole new meaning.

Throughout the evening and early morning, Marisha was more than forthcoming about her life, obviously with the intent of me reciprocating. She was 42 years old, had never married, had no children, spoke four foreign languages, and had worked for a tour agency. She did translations to earn extra money. Of course, she did not mention her former KGB ties.

I provided Marisha with a *Readers Digest* version of my life. Fifty years old, divorced, three children, a lucrative career in the private sector, and an extensive travel portfolio. Men aren't as expressive as women, I would tell her. I don't like to brag.

"Marisha, it's better you did not know everything about me so soon . . . there would be nothing left for you to explore . . . isn't part of the attraction the unknown?"

On Friday, Marisha went to the museums. I would go to the safe house in the mornings, rest up, and then meet with Matteo, my contact investigator in Prague, and his colleagues.

I would rendezvous with Marisha later in the evening, have a glass or two of my favorite wines and Marisha's usual vodka cocktail, and then retire to our room.

Sal gave me a rundown on Turgay, where he stayed in Prague, and a physical description.

Turgay was staying at the Andaz Hotel in Prague. He was 6-2, weighed about 210 pounds, had dark hair and brown eyes, and was always well-dressed. He may not have checked into the hotel under his real name. He may be using an alias.

One evening, as Marisha and I sat at the bar in The Grand Hotel, I noticed two well-dressed men chatting. Periodically they would glance our way. I, of course, assumed they were KGB/FSB. At this point, it didn't matter. If they were, perhaps I should send drinks over and say hello. Just as I had seen in the movies. I didn't.

From the bar, Marisha and I moved to a table. I told Marisha my time in Prague had been extended. A matter arose that required my immediate attention. Rather than seeming upset or angry, she was elated.

"Does that mean we can be together for another couple of weeks," she asked.

"Why not?" I responded.

After a couple of drinks and dinner, we retired to our room. The two well-dressed gentlemen were no longer at the bar; they had disappeared. There was little doubt in my mind that they were KGB/FSB.

I was cautious not to discard or leave any papers reflecting the investigation in the room. I could not use the phone to discuss any investigative issues with Sal. I knew that this might seem odd to Marisha. I would only use the phone to provide Marisha and those listening with disinformation.

As I was about to sleep, Marisha asked, "Marty, is everything okay . . . you seem distracted?"

Marisha pumped me for information I couldn't share with her.

"Everything's great, Marisha. . . . we are going to spend more time together than we anticipated . . . and if you want to go shopping tomorrow, feel free . . . the day is on me. . . ." An expense account always comes in handy.

Marisha reminisced about her life in Russia for the next hour or so. She loved her homeland and could not think of living anywhere other than Russia. She had beautiful memories of growing up as a child.

Her parents were members of the Communist Party. Her mother was a professor of languages at one of the more prestigious universities in Moscow. Her father was a renowned biochemist who had won many international awards. She was an only child. Like many who live in a gilded cage, Marisha learned at a young age that living off the earnings of others was not only a privilege but a respectable right.

There was no doubt that Marisha was well-connected to the intelligentsia. She was not about to forsake her ancestral roots for anything, especially an American.

I could feel the anxiety in Marisha. She asked too many questions, wanting to know too much about me and my life.

I would often say, "Marisha, I'm an enigma . . . don't try to figure me out . . . it's not worth your time or energy . . . enjoy the moment. . . ."

The less ammunition I gave her, the safer I felt.

Naturally, Marisha had ulterior motives. She was there to learn as much about me as she could. This would be a game of cat and mouse.

CHASING FRIENDS OF DOROTHY

It was now Saturday morning, and Marisha was excited about exclusively spending the weekend with me. Unfortunately, I was about to disappoint her. Our investigative team decided Saturday night was the best time to surveil Turgay.

Regardless of the country, weekends are productive for a covert investigative assignment.

"Marisha, I am sorry to disappoint you, but I must work on Saturday and Sunday. The people I am joint-venturing with have decided that this would be a good time to sit down and work out the details of our joint venture," I told her.

I felt the disappointment in her reaction.

"You mean I won't see you much this weekend," she responded.

"Marisha, if and when we kick off our joint venture in Russia, these are the obstacles that make life with investigators personally challenging . . . it is not conducive to maintaining a healthy, long-term relationship."

I am sure she understood that. If Marisha were former KGB, as McComb told me, she would realize that you are married to your career.

"Marisha, have you ever heard the term "unassailable mistress?"

"No," Marisha responded. "What does that mean?"

"Well, here's another idiom for your repertoire . . . the unassailable mistress is the career you choose. You dedicate your life over that of your partner or spouse . . . it is your identity, purpose, and self-fulfillment . . . it consumes you." I articulated it in the strongest of terms.

"Unassailable mistress, I have to note that one for the record . . . so I guess I'm your assailable mistress, Marty?"

We laughed. "You are," I said.

"We've spent the night together, haven't we . . . you were assailed but not assaulted . . . there's a difference." Again we laughed.

I was sure to tell her and anyone else who may have been listening that she was here of her own free will and could leave whenever she desired.

"You need three things, Marisha; a passport, a credit card, and an airline ticket . . . you are free to leave and go anywhere. . . ."

"Are you trying to get rid of me," Marisha retorted.

"Of course not, but I do want you to know that if and when you tire of this arrangement (vis-à-vis relationship), you are free to move on . . . no one owns you or me. . . ."

While I was being sharp and abrupt, I was sure her self-esteem could handle my curt response. She witnessed the unseemly parts of life as KGB. She was non-pulsed.

"You're right, Marty; no one owns you but the unassailable mistress." Touché.

Marisha was a match for me. She was quick-witted, razor-sharp, and consistently curious, so much so that it could be irritating.

What wouldn't I do for the "unassailable mistress?"

Of course, Saturday was around the corner. I needed to get my sleep. Marisha was less than accommodating. She was wound up and wanted to enjoy the night. She called the concierge and ordered a bottle of vodka and a bucket of ice.

"What kind of wine would you like, Marty,"?

"Amarone or Sassaicaia will do."

It was time to splurge. The client was footing the bill. Plus, it gave me the "street creds" that would only endear me to Marisha and her colleagues—who would soon be mine.

Saturday had arrived quicker than I thought. I planned to go to the safe house by 11 A.M., call Sal, and provide him with an update. It was 10 A.M., and I hadn't showered or had breakfast.

"Marisha, could you call room service and order breakfast. . . . I'm running late and have to meet my colleagues by noon. . . ."

"No problem, honey, will do." Marisha was taking certain liberties that I was not comfortable with.

I showered, had breakfast with Marisha, gave her a couple of hundred dollars cash, and told her to enjoy herself.

Upon arriving at the safe house, I called Sal. It was only 7 A.M. in New York, and Sal did not welcome an early morning call. Then again, Sal realized that his time was my time—his client was frantic over the situation involving Turgay. Sal's relationship with this well-paying client was reinforced by our ability to learn about Turgay and his coming and going.

"Sal, do you have Turgay's cell phone number . . . the alias he may be using at the hotel . . . any email addresses . . . any credit card numbers . . . bank accounts . . . passport numbers . . . ?

Sal was overwhelmed. "What do you need all that for," Sal asked.

"Sal, it's better that you don't know some things . . . an investigation is like making sausage . . . a lot of information, some of it useless, is collected and some discarded. . . . what is left is the finished product . . . hopefully it's what the client was looking for. . . ."

The less Sal knew about my access to the "gray market," the better. As an attorney, he had to be especially careful about using what has become increasingly privileged information. Hacking phone accounts, bank accounts, hotel records, and emails can result in criminal charges.

Nonetheless, a robust gray market can access virtually anything for the right price. As we once knew it, privacy is a thing of the past. And if it's on the internet, it's retrievable. Sal need not know too much.

Sal told me to call him back in a couple of hours. He would reach out to the client and acquire as much information as he was willing to share.

I departed the safe house and met my colleagues at their office.

In this business, relationships mean everything. Who you know is as important as what they know. The two go hand-in-hand. Sources of information can open up leads. It is the bread and butter of investigations.

Meeting with Matteo at his office, the first order of business was determining who he knew at the hotel. As a rule, the desk clerk and the concierge are two of the most knowledgeable sources.

While we knew Turgay's given name, Sal did not provide me with his surname. More than likely, Sal was protecting his client from disclosure or, perhaps, testing me to determine whether I would learn it. However, we were stymied without it unless we could ID Turgay through his physical description.

Matteo was familiar with the hotel's management.

In this business, hotel management is a critical cog in accessing all types of information—credit card information, passport data such as countries visited, phone calls made through the main switchboard, and the patron's quality of life. It is a blueprint for developing a portfolio of the person under investigation.

I contacted Sal and asked for a picture of Turgay. Within hours, Sal faxed me a picture of Turgay. He was working on acquiring the other information I had requested.

We decided to camp out in the lobby of the hotel. It was a Saturday night, and the lobby was buzzing with hotel guests. We blended into the crowd but realized that our presence would have to be as inconspicuous as possible.

We observed a tall, dark-skinned male, extremely well-dressed, enter the hotel with another man within an hour of our surveillance. It was Turgay. He proceeded to the front desk, spoke to the desk clerk, was handed a package, and got on the elevator.

Matteo went into action. He contacted his source in management. He advised him of what we had observed and asked him to make a discrete inquiry of the desk clerk in the least intrusive manner. We did not want the desk clerk to become curious or speak to Turgay about this intervention.

Within an hour, Matteo had the information.

Turgay was staying in a suite on the eighth floor. He registered as Turgay Galick. His address was in a town outside of Istanbul, Agva-Sile. A copy of his passport showed that he had arrived in Prague earlier in the week. He made telephone calls to a phone number in New York City.

We had begun to develop a portfolio on Turgay. We decided it would serve us well to have drinks and perhaps appetizers at the bar. This way, we blended into the landscape and were not so conspicuous.

Sitting at the bar, I noticed the two gentlemen from the evening before at The Grand Hotel. Either they were also registered at Andaz Hotel or following me. This was more than a coincidence. Indeed, it was eerie.

Not long after Matteo and I sat at the bar, Turgay and this other male entered the room. They sat at a table and chatted up quite animatedly. Turgay spoke fluent English, which led me to believe that his guest was English-speaking, possibly the person Turgay called in New York. He would be our next challenge.

Turgay and the English-speaking man left the bar and had the concierge summon a taxi. They departed, but not before Matteo got the registration number on the cab. Matteo was proving to be his weight in gold. His knowledge of the landscape was, without question, irreplaceable. He had the contacts, and he knew the environment. Without Matteo, I was lost.

Matteo attempted to contact a source he had at the transport authority in Prague. It was Saturday, and his contact at the authority was not working. He said he would have to wait until Monday to ascertain where Turgay was dropped off. We decided to call it an evening and meet the following day at his office at 2 P.M.

I attempted to contact Marisha at The Grand. She did not answer the phone in the room. I took a taxi to The Grand, and as I walked in, Marisha was sitting at the bar, chatting up a storm with a younger man. I walked over, kissed Marisha, and introduced myself to the fellow sitting beside her. We changed some pleasantries, and he ultimately departed.

Marisha had a little too much to drink.

"Marty, I didn't expect you back so soon . . . is everything okay," she asked.

"Yep, all good . . . my clients had made an engagement with their wives, so we decided to take an early quit," I responded.

"At least someone is not married to their job," Marisha replied agitatedly.

"You don't expect me to sit alone in the room when you are having a good time on the town, do you? . . . see what happens when you leave me alone."

It was apparent that Marisha was not happy with the situation. "Let's get dinner, and then we can talk . . . you've had too much to drink, Marisha."

I spoke with the restaurant host. He found us a table in the quiet corner. I ordered a glass of Amarone. Marisha had another vodka cocktail.

Marisha's body language signaled her displeasure with the situation. I was afraid to tell her I had to meet the clients on Sunday afternoon.

"Why couldn't I have joined you and your clients for dinner," Marisha asked.

"Marisha, it was a last-minute decision . . . they sprung it on me as the bewitching hour approached . . . I called you at the hotel, but there was no answer. . . ."

That seemed to assuage Marisha, although I felt the constraints closing in on me. Marisha was becoming increasingly aggressive and confrontational. She sensed my reluctance to share information with her. She was probably under pressure to learn more about me. Her frustrations were boiling over.

We ordered dinner. I would cancel my rendezvous with Matteo on Sunday to avoid Marisha's fury. Maybe Matteo could go to the hotel alone now that he knew Turgay? Calling him would be tricky, especially if I could not extricate myself from Marisha. Somehow I had to go to the safe house and rearrange things. Additionally, I had to call Sal to see what other information he had developed.

While eating dinner, I told Marisha we would spend all day Sunday together.

"I have to meet with the clients for an hour or two . . . they have some paperwork they want me to go over . . . Marisha."

"I could come with you, and then we could see the city . . . stop in a museum . . . or visit the Charles Bridge," Marisha said.

This was getting complicated. Perhaps it was not a good decision to meet Marisha in Prague. Sending her back to Moscow seemed like my better option. I could only keep this charade going for so long. Marisha was too skilled not to suspect something.

"Sounds good to me," I said. Marisha seemed relieved. Time for more alcohol to get her so drunk that she would have a pounding hangover the next day.

"Waiter, can you get us a bottle of your finest vodka and a bottle of Amarone, please? . . . price is not an issue. . . ."

We drank the evening away. We both had our share of alcohol, but Marisha was utterly bonkers. She could barely walk. I had to carry her to the elevator and place her in bed.

I woke up Sunday morning and saw that Marisha could not go any-where. She was suffering from a minor case of alcohol poisoning—figu-ratively. Now was my opportunity to disappear, call Sal and Matteo, and get back to the room before Marisha came to her senses.

I quietly exited the bed, put my clothes and shoes on, and left Marisha sleeping. Hallelujah, I was safe at the safe house. Time was of the essence.

I called Matteo.

"Matteo, I need a favor . . . can you surveil Turgay yourself or with a colleague of yours . . . and can you draft up an agreement that appears to represent a joint venture between your agency and mine . . . sooner you can have it ready, the better . . . I have a short window to pick it up. . . ."

"No problem, Marty . . . I will have my colleague Giuseppina join me on the surveillance . . . she will also draft the agreement. . . . where can we meet," Matteo asked?

"Let's meet at the Andaz in two hours."

I then called Sal. Again it was early Sunday morning. He was not a welcoming voice on the phone.

"Marty, couldn't this wait till Monday," Sal asked.

"Want to keep you updated, Sal. . . . the time difference is not con-ducive to making this convenient for either of us . . . We are getting good information on Turgay, and I'm working on the phone number in New York . . . that will tell us a lot . . . I suspect it is the person I saw Turgay with at the hotel . . . we're on our way to getting you some answers. . . ."

Sal seemed happier.

Subscribers of phone numbers were relatively easy to obtain in the 90s. The gray market has tightened up today, making it risky and chal-lenging. I contacted my gray-market source in Florida and provided him with the New York phone number. He was not pleased to get a call early Sunday morning but eventually made up for it in his bill.

I immediately proceeded to the Andaz Hotel, awaiting Matteo and Giuseppina. Upon seeing Giuseppina, I wanted to send Matteo back to my hotel room and surveil with Giuseppina. She was the perfect beard for this assignment. Beautiful, to the point that she might be more of a distraction than being able to blend in.

After being introduced to Giuseppina, Matteo and I chatted for a couple of minutes, exchanged the joint-venture draft agreement, and hurried back to The Grand Hotel. Marisha was passed out in bed.

I undressed and was about to enter the shower.

"Marty," Marisha asked, "where did you disappear?"

I should have known that not much escapes Marisha's orbit. She passed out or faked it, knowing she would catch me in a lie.

"I had to get the joint venture draft agreement I told you about last night . . . you passed out, so I figured I would get it so we can go directly to the museum and Charles Bridge.."

I showed her the paperwork. She seemed satisfied.

Marisha got out of bed. I ordered room service, and after showering, we had breakfast. All seemed to be copasetic. But I knew I was playing with a viper. Marisha could and would strike at any moment. There was no trust between us, nor should there have been.

Marisha had a particular fascination with Alphonse Mucha, an artist who had resisted Czechoslovakia's occupation by the Germans. His museum had just opened in Prague. She suggested we visit the Mucha Museum and then the Charles Bridge. Today was Marisha's day to do whatever she wanted. There was no objection on my part.

After working our way through the museum, we walked to the Charles Bridge.

Prague is a city of unbelievable beauty. The architecture is magnificent and old. Standing with Marisha on the Charles Bridge and realizing it was built in the 14th century, traversed by German and Russian soldiers who raped and pilloried the people of Czechoslovakia, was a mind-altering experience. We shared our mother countries' historical stains—a conversation that would consume our dinner.

Marisha found this small boutique restaurant. She suggested we have dinner. It was nothing fancy, but the intimacy of the décor and atmosphere attracted Marisha's attention.

"Those white-tablecloth restaurants are stuffy after a while," Marisha said. "I'd find these types of restaurants more to my liking."

It was our time alone. I could sense that Marisha was about to strike. This was going to be an inquisition, not a conversation. Then again, that was my intent, so at least we were both on the same page.

"So Marty, we were standing on the Charles Bridge. . . . what were you thinking as you looked out on the landscape," Marisha asked.

"Truthfully, Marisha, all I could think about was how the German and Russian soldiers and tanks occupied this beautiful city . . . I can't imagine what it must have been like. . . ."

Marisha was, of course, willing to engage and take the bait. "But it was Russia who liberated this country . . . that was in the days when Russia was part of a greater empire . . . ," Marisha responded.

"Indeed, it was Marisha; one brutal authoritarian government replaced with another . . . It took Gorbachev to recognize the bankruptcy of communism . . . he liberated Russia and Czechoslovakia . . . a heroic figure. . . ."

Marisha was a faithful communist. She saw Gorbachev as a traitor who destroyed the Soviet Union. There were no words that could describe Marisha's venom towards Gorbachev. "Yeltsin," she claimed, "will right Gorbachev's wrongs." Gorbachev was no hero in Marisha's eyes.

Perhaps Marisha was no different from me in this respect. We all suffer under falsehoods propagated by educational systems that marginalize our original sins. As is often said, history is written by the victorious.

Trying to de-escalate the conversation, I immediately pointed out that unrestrained capitalism, much like unrestrained socialism or communism, will always lead to wanton greed.

"Marisha, always question anything that ends in an 'ism.' It usually suggests that there *may be* something more sinister at work . . . that is why the rule of law is needed to constrain human nature's basic instincts, one being greed . . . but even then, the rule of law can be distorted, which was the case in Germany with Nazism and certainly in South Africa with Apartheid . . . there is no perfect system. Still, regardless, the law provides a level of transparency which allows for public discourse and reflection. . . ."

"Enough debating the evils and benefits of communism and capitalism, Marisha. . . . let's talk about more upbeat things."

With Monday hours away, I suggested Marisha start planning her week visiting museums and other tourist-rich locations. I informed Marisha that I had a hectic week and did not know how my schedule would play out. She said she understood, but time would tell whether she indeed did.

After finishing dinner, we taxied to The Grand Hotel. We stopped for a drink at the bar and noticed these two well-dressed men sitting there. After half an hour, we went to our room and retired.

Before I knew it, Monday morning had arrived. I ordered room service and had breakfast with Marisha. I informed Marisha that I might have to work into the early evening hours but would leave her a message if she was not in the room. She seemed fine with that and asked no questions.

I dressed accordingly and left the hotel en route to meet with Matteo and Giuseppina. Matteo had contacted his source in the transport authority. He was told that the two males who summoned the taxi on Saturday dropped them off in Prague's gay district—Vinohrady.

Sunday's surveillance proved to be a dud. Either Turgay and his partner never returned to the hotel or remained holed up in their room.

I contacted my source in Florida to ascertain the subscriber to the New York phone number Turgay had called on several occasions. It was listed to Anthony Pellegrino, who resided in Staten Island, New York. When I mentioned this to Sal, he immediately knew Pellegrino.

Anthony Pellegrino was a made member of the Columbo Mafia Family. He was involved in the gas tax scam initiated and perfected by the Russian gangsters, among other illegal ventures. His son was Rocco, a flamboyant jet-setter who lived the good life. I asked Sal if he could get a picture of Rocco to compare it to the person accompanying Turgay. Sal said he would try.

We were starting to make progress. We now knew that Turgay was involved with a mobster's son. We knew that both Turgay and his partner, who we now believe might be Rocco, frequented the gay district of Prague. We needed an answer as to why Turgay was spending so much money. Was he the victim of extortion? Was there an element of blackmail?

Matteo and Guisippina continued their surveillance of Turgay and his partner. Fortunately, I could extricate myself from the surveillance, allowing me to spend the evenings with Marisha. This allayed Marisha's suspicions—one of which I may have had a lady-friend in Prague.

By Thursday, Sal had faxed a picture of Rocco to Matteo's office. Bingo, Turgay's partner, was Rocco. There was no question about it. I advised Sal of the confirmation. He was elated. He had something substantial to tell his client. But he also had a serious dilemma. Turgay was Muslim.

This would pose a problem for Sal. He would have to broach the topic very delicately. Two days later, Sal left me a message at the hotel to call him. I waited until the next day and went to Matteo's office. There I called Sal. His words still ricochet in my head.

"Marty, the investigation is over . . . send me your bill."

Sal, the professional he was, never discussed the results of his conversation with his client. I could only assume the client's worst fears came to fruition.

"JUST WHEN I THOUGHT I WAS OUT, THEY PULL ME BACK IN"

—Al Pacino in *The Godfather*

With the investigation of Turgay completed, I was now confronted with what to do with Marisha. Do we stay in Prague longer? Take her to New York? Send her back to Moscow? Or do I go with her to Moscow? The options were daunting, as were the consequences of any decision I made.

I had no desire to return to Moscow. I felt vulnerable there, naked and at the mercy of my soon-to-be colleagues. Moscow was a cold and dreary city. Had it not been for my relationships with Gregori, Andrei, Boris, and Valery, it would have been an intolerable experience. Russia is all about "who you know." Widespread bribery is a way of life. I doubt that it will ever change. It is a culture pillaged for centuries; consequently, its people are content with authoritarian rule.

Prague offered me the opportunity to enlist the aid of Matteo and Guisippina if the need arose. I could also rely on my colleagues in London. Safety and security were of primary importance.

Marisha was quite comfortable in Prague, notwithstanding her affection for communist ideology. She certainly enjoyed the finer things in life and the freedom that democracy offered.

So much for her doctrinaire musings. Money and conspicuous consumption meant as much to Marisha as to the American robber barons.

But Marisha was not a gold-digger. She thought with her heart, not her head, about romance. Marisha was typical of a single 42-year-old. She wanted a partner who enjoyed the same things she enjoyed. She was not wedded to the almighty dollar. Marisha just wanted to live comfortably as she became accustomed to in Moscow.

I decided that we would spend at least another week in Prague. I would entice Boris, Valery, Gregori, and Andrei to join us to discuss the joint venture proposal and possibly finalize an agreement. When I suggested this to Marisha, she was elated.

That weekend, Marisha and I enjoyed all the city had to offer. There were museums, cabarets, and low-key casinos. We shared delightful conversations over dinner. The edge seemed to have disappeared. Marisha was more relaxed and agreeable. She was a joy to be with. Her attitude took a 180-degree turn—for the better.

Of course, I now had to consider the options in meeting with Valery, Andrei, Gregori, and Boris. Was it worth investing my time and money in a joint venture that may be problematic—good money or not?

Indeed, most investigations are problematic. It's the nature of the business. Addressing the problems of clients is our business. We are janitors retained to clean up messy situations. There is no reason to enlist our services unless the client is in trouble or wishes to prevent problems or mitigate personally-delicate affairs.

Russia was emerging from the Iron Curtain, and the opportunities were endless and treacherous. During my adventure with Berman, I learned that having a *roof* was not an option—it was obligatory. I was not dealing with the traditional Mafia I knew in New York. These were not your conventional Italian-American families. The notion of *mafia* was more amorphous and fluid. It was more the organization of crime than organized crime.

Viscerally intimidating was the notion that you would likely be jailed, tortured, or killed without being connected to the power structure or Kremlin hierarchy. The state was the Godfather. All the power and authority emanated from the strongmen who sat in the Kremlin. Extortion was part and parcel of the state apparatus. There was no distinction between organized crime and the state. For want of a better word, they were synonymous, indistinguishable.

This was when money flowed like the mighty Zambezi River over Victoria Falls in the springtime. There was money to be made if you were willing to take advantage of the opportunities and the risks associated with "sleeping with the enemy." It was globalization on steroids.

Nonetheless, there was no harm in meeting with Valery, Boris, Andrei, and Gregori to discuss the prospects of joint venturing. I suggested to Marisha that we invite them to Prague. She liked the idea; however, I noticed a slight hesitation when I brought up Boris. I had come to realize that Boris was Marisha's Achilles heel.

We returned to The Grand, had a cocktail or two at the bar, and then retired to our room. I told Marisha to call Boris the following day and extend the invitation. I would take care of their expenses and arrange for their lodging.

Marisha became quite anxious when I bluntly asked her, "Will Boris have a problem with you and me sharing a room?"

She hesitated and said, "Boris was not aware that I came to Prague . . . it might prove a bit uncomfortable.."

I sensed there may have been a "thing" between Boris and Marisha—I remembered her asking me not to tell Boris about the watch I purchased her.

I knew I had to confront her at that point, or this meeting was a non-starter.

"Marisha, are you and Boris having an affair," I asked. "If you are, this could be quite unpredictable and risky."

Marisha admitted they had an affair a year ago, but it was over. Boris refused to leave his wife, and she felt that the relationship was at a dead end. Nonetheless, she thought that seeing us together would inflame him.

"Marisha, let me ask you something. Were you aware of the two well-dressed men at the hotel bar? Did you see that glance over at us periodically?"

"Yes, Marty, I think they were following me . . . I do not doubt that Boris sent them to see what I was doing in Prague. . . ."

At this point, it was a no-brainer. Boris was aware of our relationship, and I may as well address it with him when he and the others arrived in Prague.

"I will call Boris and extend the invitation . . . let me address it."

Marisha seemed a bit relieved but was still apprehensive.

"How will you tell Boris you are here with me," Marisha asked.

"I needed a translator in Prague and reached out to you."

"But I never told him I would see you in Prague . . . he will be angry with me," Marisha said, trembling.

"He will not do anything to you here in Prague . . . let me try to deal with this man-to-man," I reassured Marisha.

Marisha lay in bed, her eyes staring at the ceiling. She was rapidly absorbing the complications our arrangement posed. Of course, so was I.

Sunday morning, I awoke, and Marisha was still sleeping. I knew I might have to contact Matteo, hoping he could serve as my *roof* in Prague if Boris acted up. Before we called Boris, I would reach out to Matteo.

I ordered room service. Marisha awoke, we showered and got dressed. I told her my game plan, and she was relieved.

"Marisha, my partners here in Prague, Matteo and his colleagues are well-positioned . . . If Boris has a problem, he is on their turf . . . you need not worry yourself . . . we will figure the rest out as we go along. . . ."

Of course, this did not address her concerns in Moscow when she returned. At this point, that was a can of worms that I could not untangle now.

I called Matteo and suggested we meet at his office later in the afternoon. He was more than accommodating. I did not want Marisha there, fearing that other things might come up regarding Turgay. I was sure, and given her state of mind, she would oblige me.

We would put off our call to Boris until later that afternoon, early evening, or Monday.

I tried cheering Marisha up, making jokes about what a tangled web we weave. She was trying to appear content, but underneath the façade, I could see that her return to Moscow would not be pleasant. Of course, I was also thinking about how I would gracefully extricate myself from this ugly situation.

This was turning into a nightmare.

As I departed the hotel to meet Matteo, I noticed the two well-dressed men sitting in the lobby. I glanced at them, and we made eye contact. Neither acknowledged the other, however. I do believe they knew that

I knew they were following me. I think it was on purpose that they exposed themselves to me. Perhaps it was a warning from Boris.

I met with Matteo at his office. He had a fancy cappuccino machine in his office. He asked if I wanted coffee, cognac, cigarettes, or cigars. Jokingly, I responded, "all the above."

"Ok, Marty, what's your situation," Matteo asked.

I explained the arrangement between Marisha and me. I told him that it was likely Marisha was a former KGB. He laughed. "Marty, there are no former . . . they never give up the craft . . . it's in their blood. . . ."

I told him about my anticipated joint venture with Boris, Valery, Gregori, and Andrei. His response was, "You must have a death wish . . . You should know that KGB is all over Prague . . . we are constantly running into them during our investigations . . . it's never a good thing . . . believe me."

He agreed. "However, there is plenty of money to be made as the Russians spend rather lavishly in Prague . . . If you generate a good client base, it is quite lucrative . . . but risky . . . you never know who you are truly dealing with. . . ."

I then told him about the situation involving Marisha and Boris. Again, Matteo laughed, suggesting a three-some might appeal to all of us. He was, of course, trying to lower the temperature.

"This is not going to end well," Matteo cautioned as if I didn't realize.

Matteo was pretty calm about the entire situation. He did not react like I thought he might.

"Marty, we are well connected in Prague . . . I have former KGB working with and for me . . . I'm sure we will be able to work things out . . . enjoy yourself in our beautiful city. . . ."

His words were a relief.

I returned to The Grand. The two gentlemen in the lobby were no longer there. As I was about the enter the elevator, both were leaving. Again our eyes connected. They just stared—only this time, it felt ominous. Perhaps I was reading into it? Too many spy stories?

I proceeded to the room. As I entered the room, Marisha was sobbing. "Marisha, what's wrong," I asked.

"I just met with those two gentlemen you saw in the lobby . . . they are KGB here in Prague . . . they told me that Boris was aware of my traveling to Prague and meeting with the American . . . Boris feels that I deceived him. . . ."

I told Marisha about my meeting with Matteo and that we would work things out. "Boris may be mad now, but he will get over it." Of course, I was unsure whether Boris and Marisha were setting me up. You can never trust KGB!

Now that the cat was out of the bag, I figured it would be the right time to call Valery and invite the group to Prague. We had nothing to lose.

I called Valery to arrange for him, Boris, Gregori, and Andrei to come to Prague the following week.

"Marty . . . let me make the arrangements. . . . I understand Marisha is there with you. . . ."

"Who told you, Valery?"

"Boris did. . . . He wondered why Marisha was there?"

"I needed an interpreter and asked her to join me in Prague if she wanted to make some extra money . . . It's not a big deal, Valery. . . ."

"I'm not so sure. . . . Boris felt betrayed. . . . he feels you should have contacted me and let Boris know."

"I wasn't under the impression that Marisha worked for Boris. . . ."

"Marty, remember, we are your contacts in Russia and Belarus, not Marisha . . . it is not wise to mix business with pleasure . . . it never ends well. . . ."

"Let's deal with it when you get here. . . . this is getting sickening, Valery. . . . I am not your employee . . . if you wish to bring the wives, just let me know . . . I will take care of the room arrangements. . . ."

"Valery, here is the phone number of the hotel . . . Just ask for hotel guest Martin Grimes . . . I booked the room under my name . . . By the way, Valery, would you like to speak with Marisha?

"Yes, please put her on the phone."

I handed the phone to Marisha. I whispered, "don't act scared or upset . . . be confident and take the offense . . . don't let Valery bully you. . . ."

"Hello, Valery . . . looking forward to seeing you next week . . . Hopefully, you will bring your wives . . . I'm sure they will love this city . . . safe travels, Valery."

There was no reason to back down at this point. Using Valery's favorite idiom, "to look weak is to get beat."

We left no doubt about who had the upper hand in Prague. Subtly Valery could read between the lines. If Boris was about to cause trouble over Marisha, "affairs of the heart do not end well." The message was being sent loud and clear—please, please, bring the wives.

With the air cleared, it was time for Marisha and me to soak up all Prague had to offer for the time being. Off to explore the wonders of this architecturally-riveting city that was the jewel of the Russian empire at one time.

Just as I was graciously attempting to remove myself from this vile and sinister world, I was seduced by the intrigue and darkness that consumed its' duplicitous culture. My soul had entered this world of darkness and opacity.

SHOCK AND AWE

Awaiting Valery's return call, Marisha and I retired for the evening but not before imbibing some spirits and wine. I became more amenable to vodka, and Marisha enjoyed the bold Tuscan wines with their robust alcohol content. Our alcoholic preferences started to blend.

Monday morning, Marisha and I awoke to the ringing of the phone. "Marty, this is Valery . . . I spoke with Andrei, Boris, and Gregori . . . we are thinking of joining you on Wednesday . . . does that work?"

"No problem, Valery . . . are you bringing the wives," again reinforcing the message subtly, letting Valery know it wouldn't be wise.

"Marty, we don't mix business with pleasure . . . we'll be coming by ourselves."

"No problem, Valery . . . let me know your flight, and I will have a car service collect you from the airport."

Now it was time to work out the logistics. I had to demonstrate that I was calling the shots and was not to be outnumbered or outmaneuvered by them. Matteo and Guisippina would be my aces in the hole.

I would use them as my beards to address any issues in Prague.

I would enlist their KGB associate to attend any meetings.

A "shock and awe" approach would advantage me in future negotiations.

I was not willing to return to Moscow. Prague was to be our agreed-upon rendezvous.

Then there was Marisha. What to do about her situation? There was no simple answer other than to convince Boris that Marisha was off-limits—not to be a pawn in this game of extra-marital sex. I had to know, of course, that Marisha and Boris weren't in cahoots. I would have to test Marisha's loyalty.

This would not be easy. Her KGB training and experience made her the consummate liar. She would not be foolish enough to get caught in a trap I would set. But those who deceive often deceive themselves into a false sense of immunity. I was banking on her self-confidence in lying to trip her up.

Could I have Guisepinna interrogate her and get her female intuition? This might work or at least give me some sense of comfort.

I suggested this strategy to Matteo. He agreed and felt that Guisepinna was the perfect foil. I would tell Marisha that I knew she was a former KGB operative. I needed to know that she and Boris were not engaged in some deception.

When I initially broached it with Marisha, she took a defensive posture.

"I slept with you for the last week, and now you are questioning my integrity," she responded.

"Marisha, all I am asking is for you to meet with Guisepinna and answer her questions truthfully. I need to be confident that you are with me and not with Boris. . . . let's face it, you had a long-term affair with Boris, and I can't be sure you're still not in love with him . . . I need to be reassured. . . ."

Marisha agreed, for her options were quite limited.

I arranged a meeting later in the week with Matteo and Guisepinna at his office. I introduced them to Marisha as my partners in Prague. Guisipinna was more than gracious, making Marisha feel comfortable. She invited Marisha into the office kitchen and offered her an expresso or cappuccino. They sat there while I met with Matteo.

Matteo understood the predicament I was in. It seemed he wasn't concerned about Boris or whether he would be hostile.

"Marty, understand something . . . here in Prague, we get along with KGB . . . they need us, and we need them . . . lots of Russian money is pouring into Prague . . . they want assurances that it is invested wisely if you know what I mean . . . Boris will not be a problem. . . ."

Matteo suggested that his KGB associate, Oleg attend the meeting with Valery, Andrei, Boris, and Gregori. He thought it was wise to bring Oleg, a local KGB agent with whom he worked closely.

"Oleg's presence will send the right message to Boris and his people . . . he is well-acquainted with the Moscow crew . . . I wouldn't doubt that he knows Boris. . . ."

"Matteo, I will leave it to your judgment . . . you haven't steered me wrong yet," I responded.

At this point, Guisippinna had finished speaking with Marisha. She looked at me and signaled a thumbs up. I sensed all was good, and Marisha and Boris were not conspiring against me. In this world, conspiracies are rampant.

I suggested to Matteo that the four of us go for dinner. Matteo had his favorite restaurant not far from his office. He suggested we go there. He could get a private dining area so we could talk freely.

At the restaurant, we ordered cocktails and wine. Matteo, Guisipinna, and Marisha were spirit persons. I stayed with a bottle of fine Italian wine, a Barolo. And plenty of sparkling water. This was going to be a long evening.

Matteo raised the issue of Boris and his prior relationship with Marisha. He suggested we address it head-on in private before the meeting with the others. Just Boris, Marisha, and I.

"There is no need to be bashful or embarrassed . . . Boris must understand that the past is the past and should not get in the way of making money . . . , Matteo opined.

I smiled and added, "That's exactly what Valery said to me . . . he does not mix business with pleasure . . . they will understand that. . . ."

Matteo also suggested that Oleg attend the meeting with the group of us.

In fact, "Oleg should, unannounced, walk into our dinner meeting," Matteo said.

Matteo was setting the stage for any possible blowback from Boris. It was Matteo's velvet glove that would make our day.

We then discussed the joint venture, the percentages, the client base, and the management of the processes. I was not excluding Matteo and his firm from partaking in the arrangement. He was too valuable and trustworthy.

Marisha listened. This was new to her. This was private enterprise 101. It was about profits and losses, assets and liabilities, and risks and costs. And it was about trust and character.

As the evening wore on, we decided to meet at Matteo's office the following morning before Boris and the others arrived. Oleg would be at the meeting and introduced to Marisha and me. Matteo will have alerted Oleg to the situation involving Boris and Marisha. There would be no need to rehash it.

We left the restaurant and taxied to The Grand. Marisha was grateful for Matteo's intervention. She felt that boldly confronting Boris and delicately threatening him would be sufficient. Undoubtedly, facing Boris straight on was the only approach he would understand. Boris did not need marital problems with Tanya.

Marisha slept soundly that night. She was now in our camp. At least, I thought so.

IF IT WERE EASY, THEY DON'T NEED US

Had I known that the Boris-Marisha debacle would interfere with our joint venture, I probably would have pulled the plug long ago. Now that we seem to have worked out a game plan, meeting with Boris and the others was on the agenda for later today. They were to arrive at the airport in several hours and be taken to The Grand Hotel.

Marisha and I met with Matteo, Guisippina, and Oleg at Matteo's office.

Oleg was introduced to Marisha and said, "leave it to me . . . Boris will not be a problem . . . I know him, and more to the point, I know his roof . . ."

Oleg agreed to meet us for dinner at The Grand unannounced.

That's all Oleg had to say. Marisha knew all would work out just fine.

Upon arrival at the hotel, Matteo, Guisippina, Marisha, and I greeted Boris, Valery, Andrei, and Gregori. I made the customary introductions and suggested they unpack, freshen up, and meet us for dinner in the lobby around 8 P.M. They agreed.

Matteo made a call to his friend in management. He requested a private dining room and several bottles of good vodka. This would be an expensive and libacious evening, but we felt that this was a necessary sales pitch as it was a meeting to begin working out the kinks in our joint venture.

As 8 o'clock rolled around, Boris, Andrei, Valery, and Gregori entered the dining room. We were seated at a long, rectangular table. Valery and Marisha were sitting in the middle and on both sides of the table. They would translate.

Giuseppina introduced herself, speaking fluent Russian. We explicitly told the group that speaking in Russian would not hinder knowing what they were saying.

As all the pleasantries were just about to finish up, Oleg arrived. Seeing Boris and Gregori, he immediately acknowledged them. They had served in KGB together throughout the years. It certainly surprised Boris and Gregori, but that was the point.

Now for the details. Matteo asked, "who do you conceive of your client base?"

Boris (thru Valery) responded, "we have several well-positioned investors looking to invest in overseas real estate . . . preferably in New York and Miami . . . They need due diligence to feel comfortable moving their money to the United States."

In other words, Boris needed vetted potential investment opportunities in the states to assure his clients it was safe. That seemed relatively simple.

I then told Boris that depending on the scope of due diligence, we could cost it at a flat or hourly rate. I preferred the hourly approach. As I pointed out, there are always surprises in conducting due diligence. What may begin as an open and shut investigation becomes more complicated.

I also pointed out that our clients in the states would want due diligence conducted on Boris's clients. "We have fairly strict laws on transferring money through our banking system. Our client's in the states need to be mindful of who they are dealing with. . . ."

"Our hourly rate in the New York area was $350. While it may seem high for you, anything lower would cut into our profit margins."

Of course, they were not familiar with our way of doing business. This was on-the-job training for them.

I agreed to provide the client with a proposal addressing the scope of work. All parties would sign a retainer agreement. The client would either electronically transfer the retainer to our corporate account or provide us with a cashier's check. A paper trail was necessary to avoid any legal problems.

Cash would be unacceptable as it could present us with some real problems.

"We cannot become a vehicle for laundering money on behalf of criminals, whether in Russia or the United States," I firmly pointed out.

Boris and Gregori seemed taken aback by this. I explained our laws on moving cash through our banking system and how it is a red flag to the regulators. They believed we could "expedite" the process—their word, not mine.

I then discussed how we would divide up the money. The investigators who brought the client on board would receive an origination fee. After all, costs are accounted for; the fee would be twenty percent of the profits. In other words, twenty percent of the net and not the gross of any due diligence. Unfamiliar with the terms "net" and "gross," I explained the difference.

I pointed out that every investigation has payable costs above the hourly rate. For example, hotel and travel expenses, access to digital sources, human asset costs, etc. These costs exclude the "net" profit; hence the originator is not compensated. These represent the "gross." Again, a tutorial on the pricing ratios involved in conducting due diligence.

If there were a hesitation between Boris and the others, Matteo, Guisippina, or Oleg would interrupt and try to clarify the confusion.

I remember Oleg saying, "if you wanna do business in the Western world, you better understand where you will get into trouble with the police," a warning to Boris and the group. Knowing your environment is the same in the United States as in Russia. The authorities drive the processes—formalized laws in the United States and bribery in Russia.

I responded jokingly, "the two may not be that different."

I suggested we draft an agreement between my firm and Boris's investigative entity and enter a formal agreement. Matteo agreed to initiate the process the following day.

As the evening ended, we all shared a toast—cognac—to our future joint venture.

Oleg, Boris, Valery, Gregori, and Andrei stepped aside. Oleg was taking care of business—Marisha's business. The invisible hand was at work.

Matteo and Guisipinna departed. And Marisha and I retired to our room. We agreed to await a call from Matteo and meet again on Monday to finalize the joint venture.

Once in the room, Marisha seemed more at ease. She didn't have to engage in the laborious task of interpreting and was out of Boris's presence.

"Marisha, now it's time to relax . . . Oleg is handling any blowback you will get from Boris . . . to use another American idiom, "the ship may have left the port, but a skilled captain is navigating the currents. Oleg is that captain."

THE CLASH OF CULTURES

On Monday, late afternoon, I received a call from Matteo. He finalized the joint venture agreement. We could meet in his office on Tuesday, and all sign on to the deal. We decided on 11 A.M.

Boris and the group were preparing to leave on Wednesday morning. I intended to go on Thursday. Marisha posed an issue. Does she return to Moscow with Boris and the group, leave on Thursday for Moscow, come to New York with me, or stay in Prague? There were no appealing options.

As I surveyed the landscape, I came to one conclusion. Marisha had to return to Moscow. Her life and her heart were planted there. Happiness is not defined by who you are with or where you are. At peace with your inner self —contentment—is the only valid barometer.

Her culture was not only antithetical to the West; it was paradoxical and resentful to Western values. She would never find happiness in the West, especially since she came from Russia's aristocracy, where privilege was part of her DNA. At this stage in her life, *"starting over"* was out of the question. Marisha had no idea what it was like to make a living or career absent the accouterments the Communist Party afforded her.

That evening, Marisha and I decided to have dinner by ourselves. I was "translated out." I wanted to discuss with Marisha her thoughts and, of course, mine.

We found an intimate restaurant not far from the hotel that didn't have white tablecloths. I could tell that Marisha was sad. She knew that our time together was about to end. I delicately encouraged her to return to Moscow and find what makes her happy.

"Remember, Marisha; you can never compete with the unassailable mistress . . . you have to find what makes you content . . . what fulfills your needs and desires . . . it can never be material things . . . I am a material thing . . . today it's me; tomorrow, it is someone else . . . in the end, only you can find happiness within yourself . . . not thru someone else . . . if you learn one thing, Marisha, the person that can make you happy, can also make you sad . . . find your inner peace. . . ."

I suggested to Marisha that I put her on my payroll as my representative from Russia. You would interface with Boris and Gregori in Moscow and Andrei and Valery in Minsk. Given their past, Marisha was unsure whether she and Boris could have a working relationship.

"Time, Marisha, heals all wounds is another idiom for your repertoire."

As the evening progressed, our conversation meandered all over. Neither of us wanted the time to pass. We wanted to be frozen in the moment.

But the reality was creeping upon us. Time to return to the hotel and make the final arrangements for Marisha's return to Moscow.

I asked Marisha to accompany me to the airport on Thursday and return to Moscow. She was on board with that suggestion, although I was sure she was plotting another plan. For all her love for Russia and its culture, Marisha knew that things had changed under Yeltsin. It was not the Russia she knew nor the one she chose to remember. Marisha's life would be changed immeasurably, so why not start over in a more hospitable environment?

We woke up on Tuesday morning, and the sky was gray and dreary. So were our moods. The hours ticked away. We were meeting Matteo in his office at 2 P.M. We ordered room service, finished breakfast, showered, and went to Matteo's office. We arrived an hour early.

Enjoying a cappuccino with Matteo, he asked Marisha, "So what are your plans?"

Marisha responded that she was returning to Moscow. "Are you sure you wanna go back? What if I offered you a position with my firm? Would you stay here in Prague?"

I immediately saw a change in Marisha. She was much more talkative and collaborative. "What would I do, Matteo?"

"I always need interpreters . . . with all the Russian money and businesses here in Prague. I could use you in many ways . . . believe me, you will work . . . and make money, of course."

As the conversation continued, Boris and the group arrived. Matteo presented us with the agreement translated into Russian and English. We read it and signed it. Our joint venture was off to a start.

Matteo broke out his cognac, and we again toasted a successful future. Boris and the group departed. I told Valery that I would see them off tomorrow.

"Will Marisha be joining us," Valery asked.

"I don't think so, Valery. Marisha will be working with Matteo and his firm in Prague. He offered her a position, and she accepted," I responded.

While it was undoubtedly presumptuous and misogynistic on my part to make Marisha's decision, it provided Marisha with a graceful exit strategy. She thanked me later for making a decision she struggled with.

Matteo, Guisippina, Marisha, and I went to dinner; Guisipinna welcomed Marisha on board. Matteo discussed the logistics of Marisha relocating and traveling between Moscow and Prague.

Matteo's velvet glove once again came thru. As did Oleg's iron fist!

"Marisha, you will learn a lot from Matteo and Guisipinna . . . notice the velvet glove . . . and don't forget the unassailable mistress . . . both will become part of your repertoire."

Problem solved. Marisha did not have to leave Russia or work with Boris. Oleg would be her *roof* if Boris acted up. Marisha could come to New York periodically. And I could visit Prague, hopefully with a client footing the bill.

When we returned to The Grand, I could see the joy in Marisha's eyes. She couldn't believe this all came together after a simple meeting in Moscow months earlier.

You can never predict where life's adventures and opportunities will bring you. You can embrace the future or live in the past. Marisha chose both worlds.

I met with Boris, Andrei, Gregori, and Valery on Wednesday morning. We had breakfast, and their car service transported them to the airport.

We agreed to speak the following week, as I had a client needing advice regarding an investment opportunity.

Marisha and I shared dinner again on Wednesday night. I was departing on Thursday morning. This would be our opportunity to discuss her future. The unassailable mistress was awaiting my return.

I reassured Marisha that she was up to any task Matteo gave her; she would do well in a market economy. She was to listen and learn from the master magician, Matteo, who could make problems vanish. She was in for the ride of her life.

Thursday morning, as she lay in bed, I kissed Marisha goodbye. I promised we would meet again.

Wheels up and over the Big Pond, I flew.

LET THE GAMES BEGIN

It all began when Valery told me that Boris had a client in Moscow who had a family member in the United States involved with the Russian Orthodox Church in New York City. Immediately my antennae were alerted. So I listened as Valery outlined the proposal.

A patriarch or priest in New York had proposed to Boris's client that a real estate reclamation project in New York was searching for investors. His name was Ivan Portonosky. Valery asked me if I could conduct due diligence on Portonosky. Valery would obtain the name of the project.

I advised Valery that I would send him a proposal and a retainer agreement. In it, Boris's client would post a $10,000 retainer to initiate the due diligence.

The following week I received the signed retainer agreement and a cashier check for $10,000. Gennady Rostov, a real estate investor in Moscow, signed the agreement. According to Valery, Rostov was considered a distressed real estate investor (i.e., bottom feeder) who made his money through state loans to refurbish deteriorated housing in and around Moscow.

Rostov was a second cousin of Portonosky, who visited him in Moscow the year before. This allowed Rostov to expand his portfolio now that the Iron Curtain had fallen. Investment opportunities outside of Russia were considered safe investments. Capital flight on a massive scale heralded a new and robust industry—money laundering.

Investment in real estate was one of the protected methods of moving money outside Russia. It was one of the several methods of exchanging Russian capital for real estate with no questions. There were no requirements such as "know your customer," "cash reporting rules," or "suspicious transaction reports."

A five million dollar cash payment for a mansion in London, Manhattan, or Miami raised no red flags among the financial sector regulators. It was perfectly legal and spurred the real estate market—perhaps in ways not conducive to a good supply and demand model.

There was certainly nothing illegal in Rostov's ambitious efforts to expand his portfolio. He was simply an investor looking to capitalize on new investment opportunities. Portonosky offered him such an opportunity. Boris, his group, and my firm were managing the risk through appropriate due diligence.

Once we had information on the reclamation project, it was apparent that government subsidies and loans were available to the investors. This alone would require a rigorous level of financial transparency. Rostov would be examined to determine whether he had the financial capital to undertake this project. The federal, state, and city governments would scrutinize his financials. This added another level of transparency to Rostov's proposal.

Determining the source of Rostov's capital would be an arduous task. Its genesis was in Russia. There was no way for the United States government to determine whether these monies resulted from illegal activity—prohibited arms trading, human smuggling, prostitution, or narcotics. Ironically, tax evasion or fraud would not have been a recognized disqualifier.

However, what proved to be compelling was Rostov's relationship with Yelstin. Doing business in Russia required meaningful and powerful political relationships. As has been said repeatedly, Russia was a mafia state, with the president the ultimate arbiter of "who gets what."

During the 90s and early 2000s, the alliances between the private and public sectors were one giant blur. Everybody had their hands in someone's pocket. And the president had his hand in everybody's pocket. It was a feeding frenzy; there was no other way to describe it.

My only concern was to ensure that Rostov had the financial capital to undertake this project, was not arrested or imprisoned for a capital crime, possessed the relevant and appropriate paperwork to leave Russia and enter the United States, and had the resources to take this project on.

Indeed, his relationship with Portonosky was a good sign. Portonosky's relationship in the real estate community was rock-solid. He had a cadre' of developers Rostov could leverage, providing them with the capital to undertake this multi-million dollar reclamation project.

Portonosky also was well-positioned politically. He had relationships with City Hall and Albany and the Federal government's housing authority. Rostov politically covered his bases in Russia and the United States. This was a match made in heaven, no pun intended.

Once given the go-ahead, Valery contacted Boris. Naturally, Boris was delighted. He would receive the origination fee of twenty percent plus whatever hours he devoted to his end of due diligence.

Our first project together was a success. No hiccups.

I contacted Matteo and appraised him of our success. He laughed and said, "risk mitigation is something the Russians thoroughly understand . . . don't count your chickens before they hatch. . . ."

I immediately thought of Marisha. Here is another valuable idiom for Marisha's expanding vocabulary. I asked Matteo whether Marisha was there.

"Of course she is. You want to speak with her?"

Marisha got on the phone. I asked her how it was going there.

"Fine, Matteo is an encyclopedia of information . . . I am learning so much . . . you were right about the market economy . . . it drives you to work . . . your mistress is my master. . . ."

We laughed. Marisha hit her stride. I knew Marisha would be a quick study. I knew Matteo was the perfect fit. I was so happy for Marisha.

"Marisha, have you gone back to Moscow?"

"Only once, Marty . . . had to bring some personal things to Prague . . . I have a beautiful apartment several blocks from the office . . . I ride my bike to work every day . . . trying to stay fit—the food is my downfall . . . and Matteo likes his spirits, so we usually end the day with drinks. . . ."

"When am I going to see you, Marty?"

"I'm quite busy . . . my mistress just won't leave me alone. . . ."

She laughed. Hopefully, she had found her inner self.

"Talk soon, Marisha . . . never know when I might just show up on your doorstep."

"Please do," Marisha responded.

Rostov was to arrive in New York over the next few weeks. I told Valery I would collect him and bring him to his hotel. Valery didn't think that would be necessary. He advised me that Rostov spoke fluent English and had friends in Brighton Beach he would likely visit and settle in with.

Of course, once I heard Brighton Beach, the bells went off. Who would he visit in Brighton Beach? Who were these "friends." Should I pursue this or leave it alone?

I suggested to Valery that we should consider surveilling Rostov. Valery saw that as detrimental to our relationship with him. "Who's paying for the surveillance," Valery asks. Rostov?"

He, of course, had a point. But my concern was whether Rostov was involved with the Russian mobsters that virtually owned Brighton Beach. This unrelenting stereotype was a fixation.

"Once shame on you, twice shame on me," another idiom for Marisha!

I could not push it out of my head. This could be a situation in which I am holding the bag if things go awry. It was my due diligence that gave Portonosky a "thumbs up."

I'll have to suck up the costs and do some more homework.

LIFE'S A BEACH

Dasha, where are you when I need you?

Back to Brighton Beach, I must go.

Memories of my time spent in "Little Odessa" are complicated. Its mystique lies in all the conspiracy theories hatched there. Who's competing with who? Who's connected with who? Who's involved in healthcare fraud? Who is involved in stock fraud and "pump and dumps?" Who is involved in arms trading, drug trafficking, and human smuggling? Brighton Beach is a kaleidoscope of crime. Everything is about relationships!

Brighton Beach is nothing like the real Russia to many of my Russian colleagues. It is infested with the low life of society. It is a caricature of the cultured, sophisticated, and well-educated Russian. It makes a mockery of what it is to be Russian.

The Russians I have had the privilege of knowing and socializing with are nothing like that portrayed in movies like *Little Odessa*. Nonetheless, ignoring this sliver of society obfuscates the so-called "queer ladder of social mobility" immigrant groups climbed as they assimilated into American culture.

I, of course, had a significant problem. I had no idea what Roskov looked like, where he was staying, who he was visiting, or a phone number. If I ask Valery for personal information, it will alert him to my intentions.

Asking too many questions in this tight-knit community would only expose me and cause problems. My partners in this joint venture, Boris and Valery, would be furious. It would likely be the end of our relationship.

There was an option that did come to mind. It was Marisha. She was well-connected among Moscow's political elites. Or Oleg? Might they know Roskov?

I wasn't sure whether to trust Oleg with this information. He was close with Boris and Gregori. Marisha, on the other hand, was loyal to me. She would not double-cross me. Fingers crossed.

I called Marisha and told her the situation. She quickly envisioned an opportunity to travel to New York and assist me with the investigation. For many reasons, Dasha being one, this was not a good idea. It would be another debacle I didn't need.

"Marisha, I need a picture of Gennady Rostov. He is a well-connected real estate developer in Moscow . . . I'm sure you may have friends that know him . . . A recent newspaper picture would do . . . a ribbon-cutting picture. . . ."

"Let me see what I can do . . . are you asking your mistress, or is this on behalf of the unassailable mistress," Marisha jokingly said.

"Ok, Marisha, I owe you . . . thanks."

I contacted Dasha and asked her if she would be available. I needed a beard again, and she was perfect in this community. "No problem. Weekdays or weekends, Marty?"

Dasha finally met a cultured Russian man from Ukraine who she was dating and living with on and off. Her weekends were usually filled with either family events or spent with her beau. I was not sure how he would take to my intervention. But I had no time to think about it. I needed Dasha whenever!

"Dasha, I have no idea just yet, but I'll take well care of your time if you could be on call." Dasha was right there when it came to earning a buck or two.

In the meantime, I awaited a call from Marisha. I did not want to do anything that might jeopardize the inquiry I was about to undertake. The invisible hand was at work.

Several days later, I received a call from Marisha. "Marty, I have your picture and much more."

"Marisha . . . you are a God-send."

"A what," Marisha asked.

"A person sent from heaven . . . Another idiom for your vocabulary."
I wasn't even sure whether she believed in God. I suspect not.

"Do you want me to bring this picture to you?"

"Marisha, a faxed picture will do . . . and any other information you have."

"Ok, I'll send you my bill as well."

Marisha was a quick study. The grass didn't grow under her feet. Oh, another idiom to give her.

Within minutes, the picture, Roskov's associates in Moscow, and a copy of his passport were in my possession. Privacy does not exist in Russia, as Boris brazenly told me.

Besides Roskov's picture, Marisha ensured I knew who I was dealing with. Roskov was intimately involved with Yelstin's family. He routinely met with his family members. He wined and dined with the political elite. "Marty, you're dealing with a real player."

Boris told me, "relationships mean everything in Russia . . . it's not what you know, but who you know."

I had to determine when Roskov was arriving in New York. Now that I had his passport, my contact in Florida could ascertain the airline and flight he would board. But it wasn't going to be cheap. This inquiry required magic.

He routinely and constantly checked the visa registry and flights from Moscow to JFK in New York. Once Roskov boarded the plane, he could tell me when he landed. I could follow his route to Brighton Beach or wherever he was staying.

It was the beginning of a new investigation that I was now doing *pro bono.*

As I sat reflecting on my career, I started questioning whether it was worth the money I made and would make with Boris and our joint venture. A lot of drama, distrust, and duplicity!

With Roskov in New York, I was now positioned to assess his legitimacy and whether he was part of Yelstin's kleptocracy.

Boris and Gregori, I was convinced, had no genuine interest in where Roskov acquired his money. Their only interest was making the origination fee and their hourly rate. It was up to me to determine if he was skirting our laws concerning money laundering or other civil or criminal activity. I was risk-averse to being embroiled in more money laundering dramas.

I contacted Dasha after I heard from my guy in Florida. Roskov would land at JFK in 5 hours. He was on a Delta Airlines flight from Moscow to JFK. I asked Dasha if she could meet me in two hours and drive to JFK Airport. Conducting surveillance with a male and female was likely to be less distinguishable. She agreed.

We drove to JFK Airport. I gave Dasha a picture of Roskov. She waited in the baggage section of the international terminal until she recognized him. He exited the front door, and a black Mercedes collected him. Dasha captured the plate number. Now I have more information to follow up on.

We followed the Mercedes to an address in Brighton Beach. Again, more information to digest.

Roskov exited the Mercedes, and the driver collected Roskov's luggage from the trunk. He carried both suitcases into the house. We decided to stay put and see if any other vehicles arrived.

Within two hours, three other late-model cars arrived. We were able to obtain the registrations from the vehicles. More information to consume.

They remained in the house until the early evening, 8 o'clock or so. They then departed to a local restaurant and joined a larger group. The restaurant owner put a "closed" sign on the door. This was a private dinner for Roskov's guests only. More license plates to capture.

We decided to call it a night. I dropped Dasha off at her house and proceeded to my office. There I called my guy in Florida. "I need several license plate look-ups. . . . can you retrieve them in a day or two?"

"I'll do my best. . . ."

By Saturday, I had the names of those who met with Roskov. I called Mike Savage and ran their names past him. His response was earth-shattering. "You hit a home run with bases loaded in the bottom of the ninth, Marty. . . . these are the real deal. . . . the Brighton Beach mafia—how'd you do it?"

"Luck, Mike . . . There's an old saying; I'd rather have luck than skill . . . In this case, I had both."

Roskov was playing with the big boys. He was not some real estate schlep who invested in distressed properties. He was here to launder money, most likely on behalf of his friends in Moscow. My partners misled me.

Marisha got her revenge—served cold!

The question now was, where do I go from here?

Do I play along or extract myself from the situation? Again, curiosity got the best of me. It also killed the cat!

Tools of the KGB

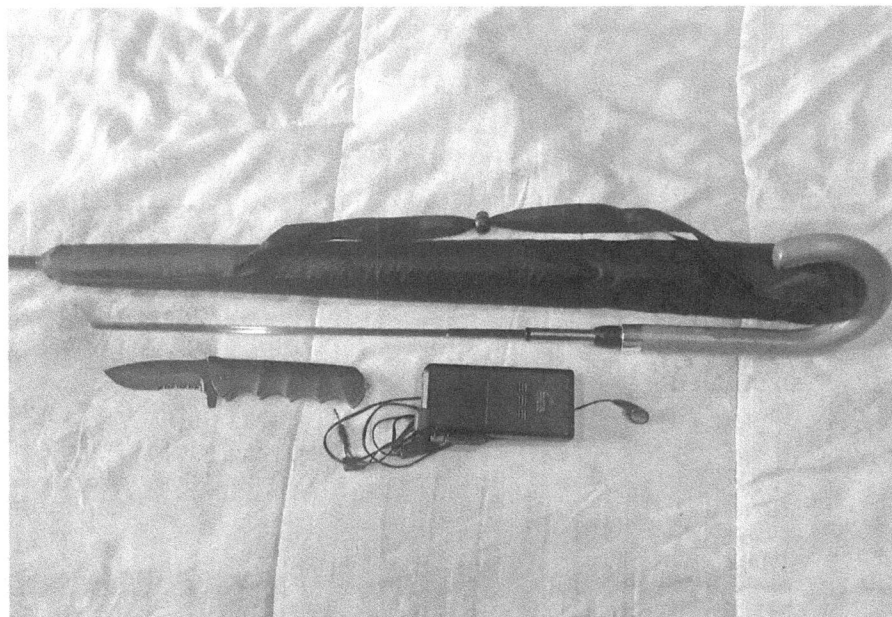

Maximillian's mansion in Cornwall

Midnight Express from Moscow to Minsk

The Unconquered Man: Haunting War Memorial

Grimes at KGB Office

Khatyn Memorial

Grimes in Moscow at KGB headquarters

Grimes's credentials

VERIFY BUT NEVER TRUST

I contacted Dasha and asked her if she would be available to conduct several surveillances in Brighton Beach. She was more than eager to get going. Making money was undoubtedly part of Dasha's DNA. Spending it on boring and cost-adverse surveillance was not necessarily part of mine.

I had to devise some plan to get Roskov to invest more money in due diligence. Valery and Boris would be more than happy to generate more billable hours. I suggested to Valery that before Roskov gets involved with any real estate moguls or construction companies in New York, he should consider conducting due diligence. There are plenty of scam artists in a city of eight million people.

Valery agreed. He would run it past Boris and have Boris sell it to Roskov. Of course, Boris and Valery knew Roskov was in New York and chose not to tell me. Regardless, I knew at this point that my colleagues in Russia were not likely to share what they had learned about Roskov. As former KGB, they had to know about his dealings with the political elites of Moscow and his connections with Yelstin.

While awaiting word from Valery, I contacted Dasha and arranged to drive to Brighton Beach in the late morning. We would surveil the house Roskov was staying at and follow him wherever he might go if and when he left. Of course, we had to be extremely careful. We did not want Roskov to suspect a tail.

Roskov's day would begin around 11 A.M. His routine was predictable. Meetings with the real estate developers and construction companies, followed by a late lunch with various Brighton Beach "heavies," then back to the house where he was staying, and then an evening on the town.

Where Portonosky fit into Rosko's plans was still a mystery. He did not attend the meeting with Roskov, suggesting that he was not necessarily the go-between we initially suspected. Perhaps he was just a beard for Roskov, giving him an excuse to visit New York to visit family and friends? Maybe his "friends" in Moscow were not privy to Roskov's "friends" in Brighton Beach?

Roskov may have kept his two worlds separate, adding another layer of conspiracy thoughts. There was no way of knowing. My colleagues in Moscow and Minsk were of little help. If they knew, they were not telling. Welcome to their world—a world of underlying and overlapping conspiracies.

Within a day, Valery contacted me. He gave me the go-ahead to conduct due diligence on the real estate developers and construction companies. I told Valery I would need the names of the companies and developers from Roskov, and we should have him sign a forty-thousand-dollar retainer agreement.

This was in the financial interests of Boris and Gregori insofar as they would be getting an origination fee (minus costs, of course) for merely selling the due diligence package to Roskov.

Capitalism works, I'm sure they were thinking.

"Not a problem. Roskov agreed that whoever he worked with in New York needed to know their pedigrees . . . New York is a big city . . . you never know who is a crook and who is honest. . . ." Valery repeated my concerns.

I received the $40,000 cashier's check-in overnight mail two days later. I now had at least $32,000 to conduct due diligence on the companies. There was little doubt in my mind that Roskov was running a counter-intelligence operation—a trick I was taught working for Berman earlier.

If I had learned nothing more from my interactions with the former KGB, it's that they trust no one, not even each other. They all have a personal agenda. Having Matteo as a sounding board, Marisha as a check and balance, and Palmisano and Savage as local resources provided me with a modicum of comfort. But I knew never to let my guard down. Mistakes in this business could be costly in any number of ways.

In dealing with KGB, there are no rules. The rules are spontaneous as situations evolve. They are solely based on personal interests; who benefits, who loses, and who is expendable. Loyalties can be fleeting. It's what always bothered me in my relationship with Marisha. What would she do to me over something more rewarding if she could deceive Boris over, of all things, a watch?

You learn quickly who has your back and is likely to mislead you. Valery, Boris, Andrei, and Gregori were not trustworthy as partners but great rainmakers. Money drove them. Loyalty was an American fairy tale.

Marisha, on the other hand, was driven by romance and love. Her capital was not, as a rule, money. Instead, Marisha needed to feel she had a soul mate, someone she could trust and depend on.

I would often tell Marisha that there are wants and needs in life. Want is freedom; need is a crutch. Take your pick, but realize both come with a cost. Freedom is not free, and need restricts freedom. I'm not convinced she ever understood it.

I never tried to figure out Oleg. He was Matteo's problem. But he was indeed an asset when we needed him. What he told Boris, I will never know. But he seemed to have resolved the situation for the moment, anyway.

Now my dilemma was how to address another money laundering scheme Roskov was about to initiate was? Investing Russian money in New York real estate was no crime, provided its origins were not illicit. Tax evasion in Russia is not a crime in the United States. It is welcomed and generously rewarded in America.

On the other hand, if these monies originated from illegal arms trading, drugs, human trafficking, extortion, or a bevy of other crimes, it could and would prove problematic here in the states.

My dilemma was simple; was working for Roskov enabling him to carry out a scheme to launder money? This was not my first rodeo. But it was on a scale I had never before encountered. Am I too far in to get out or too far out to be implicated?

As I was pondering this equation, I received a call from Savage. He knew the characters I had identified as Roskov's "friends" in Brighton Beach.

"Marty, you know those names you ran past me last week . . . well, the feds (FBI) are interested in them as well . . . I got a call from an agent . . . she wanted to know what I knew about a Gennady Roskov . . . wasn't Roskov your client?"

The FBI had picked up conversations on Roskov and his trip to the United States. I could only assume that my name was captured in the conversations intercepted. My decision was simple: cease and desist—no need to be the subject of an FBI investigation.

"Yea, Michael (Savage) . . . He has me conducting due diligence on some real estate developers and construction companies he is soliciting for a rehabilitation project in Brooklyn . . . I guess I will pass on this due diligence?"

"I wouldn't, Marty, conduct the due diligence as you would for any other investor . . . there's nothing you're doing that's illegal . . . document everything if it blows up on you . . . the FBI may visit you at some point, and you want your ducks in order . . . if you back out now, it might look suspicious to Roskov and the FBI. . . ."

"Okay, Michael, but I'm not comfortable . . . I've been here before, and this never ends well . . . seems like anytime you touch a Russian client, you end up embroiled in some scam . . . is it in their DNA or what, Michael?"

Michael laughed. "Marty, when you're brought up deceiving your government as a way of life, can you ever change? . . . it's the nature of their environment . . . as much as we see them as criminals, they see themselves as victims . . . the much-quoted Russian proverb, 'they pretend to pay us, and we pretend to work' is how they've been conditioned . . . it will take generations to bleed this mentality out of them. . . ."

I found this an unwarranted and degrading stereotype. The Russians I knew were no more dishonest than the Americans I knew. They abided by the law, looked down upon the financial fraud artists, and loved their homeland as much as any American I knew. Maybe I lived in a bubble?

Then again, maybe we all live in a bubble. Perhaps all governments lie to the people? Perhaps the term "fake news" is our reiteration of Russian propaganda. Maybe Horatio Alger's "rags to riches" was no more than capitalist fiction. Maybe that mansion on the mountain required more than just hard work. Maybe there was a lot of luck? Yea, perhaps we all live in a bubble.

Fortunately, as luck would have it, Roskov and his confederates were indicted for money laundering by the Federal government. His exploits led the FBI to the inner circles of Yelstin's family. It implicated members of Moscow's political elites—people Marisha knew and within her orbit.

Marisha contacted me when she heard about the arrests.

"Marty, I'm sure you were right in the middle of this. My information was good, wasn't it?"

"Marisha, it's not over yet. . . . there's another aspect to it that is unthinkable . . . can you believe the Russian Orthodox Church may have been defrauded by Roskov too?

"Marty, why do you find that shocking . . . the Russian Orthodox Church has always been an arm of the Kremlin and the communist party . . . who would suspect the church of laundering money? Is it any different from the Vatican . . . ?

Marisha had a point. I never thought about it. In retrospect, it makes perfect sense. A bit like the Red Cross and KGB?

A MATCH MADE IN PRAGUE

With the indictments of Roskov and his minions making international news, it was inevitable that Matteo would reach out to me.

"Marty, were you involved in that money laundering scheme that just hit the papers? Wasn't Ruskov your client? Didn't Marisha do some work for you on him? . . ."

"Yea, Matteo . . . once again, a Russian client becomes the subject of a money-laundering investigation . . . Is there ever clean due diligence on a Russian that doesn't end up in some financial boon dongle? . . . This seems to be their never-ending saga or signature crime?"

After discussing this with Matteo, I asked how Marisha was doing. He indicated that he and Marisha were now living together. I was shocked. Marisha never told me, and I had just spoken with her.

"Seriously, you and Marisha are together?"

"Marty, why are you so shocked?"

"I guess I never saw you as the committed type . . . I knew Marisha wanted a commitment, but I told her again that the unassailable mistress would never allow her to sweep me off my feet . . . being married to our careers can never be replaced by a woman, a significant other. . . ."

Matteo just laughed quite heartedly.

"Marty, Marisha told me your outlook on love and marriage . . . wasn't there a song like they go together like a horse and carriage . . . well with Marisha, we go together like a horse and carriage . . . We both love the same things, theatre, museums, travel, music, and guess what, she loves the unassailable master, me . . . it's all good, Marty. . . ."

I was happy for Marisha. Hopefully, she found her inner peace. I asked Matteo if I could speak with Marisha. "Of course, Marty."

Marisha got on the phone. I naturally congratulated her. She was a bit reticent, thinking I might be upset that she and Matteo were an item.

"Marisha, why didn't you tell me? Why did I have to hear from Matteo?

"Marty, I didn't want to be the one to tell you . . . you know I still have feelings for you?

"Marisha, remember what I told you about being committed and how a career interferes with a relationship?"

You mean the unassailable mistress and how you loved your work . . . can I give you something to think about, Marty?"

"Of course, Marisha."

"Don't love something or somebody that doesn't love you back . . . the unassailable mistress will never love you . . . the unassailable mistress is only in it for the money . . . there's more to your inner peace than money or material things it buys . . . I found my inner peace thanks to you, Marty. . . ."

Marisha was so insightful, quick-witted, and practical. She hopefully found her inner peace with Matteo. I told Marisha I would like to be invited to the wedding if they were to marry.

I told Matteo I would like to be the best man—provided he does not hold their relationship against me.

"Remember, Matteo; there are no former KGB. They are always KGB!" It has many faces.

He laughed, as did I.

It was the perfect ending for the "threesome." Or so I thought?

BINGO!

Roskov, unbeknownst to his "friends" in Russia, had another side business that garnered him monies that he did not share with his *roof* in Moscow. It involved his cousin, Ivan Portonsky, the leader of the local parish in Brighton Beach.

Portonosky's parish ran a weekly bingo event that raised money for financially distressed families. It ingratiated the church, the local community, and the political movers and shakers.

A relatively benign form of legalized gaming, bingo generates more than two billion dollars yearly in revenue. Charitable organizations and nonprofits primarily run it. A game of chance, bingo has a worldwide following for many reasons.

Usually, the money derived from the attendance fees is, among other expenses, redistributed as prize money. Most of the funds pay for ancillary services, administrative costs, and food and beverages for the participants.

Each state regulates bingo operations, often under a consumer protection agency instead of a gaming commission. The federal government has little to no say in the regulation of bingo. This, in effect, allows states to regulate the game as they see fit.

For example, one state may require a thirty percent return to the charitable organization, while another may only require a ten percent or less return.

Auditing bingo operators raises many questions about the accuracy of these audits. First and foremost, who is doing the auditing? Usually, a low-level government auditor is looking to see whether the numbers add up. Or whether the charitable organization received the return required under the respective state's regulation.

Few states assign forensic auditors to pursue bingo frauds. Consequently, seldom are bingo operators found to violate a state's laws. Most audits return unremarkable results.

Indeed, with crime rampant in cities across the country, international arms and drug trafficking, and the human slave trade (i.e., prostitution) capturing the western world's attention, bingo certainly did not rate high on the overall scale of social harms. Unless you understand how money laundering is essential in completing the cycle—from one of dirty money to that which is cleansed and circulating in the licit economy.

Roskov envisioned a win-win situation that provided Portonosky with a steady stream of revenue that often proves elusive or unpredictable for non-profits, charitable, and religious organizations.

Roskov presented Portonosky "with an offer he couldn't refuse." If Portonosky allowed Roskov to "run money through the bingo operation," Roskov agreed to pay a ten percent "referral fee" to Portonosky.

Once Roskov could insinuate himself in the church's financial operations, the games—not only bingo—began. I'm not sure they hadn't started earlier, but that discussion is for another time.

Administrative costs began to sky-rocket, with monies paid to no-show "volunteers," who were Roskov and Portonosky's "friends" and relatives. Doctored books avoided any "red flags" that the state auditors might uncover.

Costs for food and beverages also began to climb significantly. Vendors who again were "friends" and family chose to submit fraudulent invoices, exaggerating the price of the "fabricated refreshments" that never found their way to the church.

What began as a ten percent "referral fee" was ultimately whittled to less than two percent. Ruskov found a relatively bullet-proof "front" to launder money with little chance of his "friends" in Moscow learning about it.

As expected, the plot behind the plot and brilliantly executed conspiracies never end.

In many respects, bingo conducted under the auspices of religion was the ultimate scam. This was *untouchable* in a country constitutionally protecting the separation between church and state.

And Protonosky's bingo operation was just one of the thousands of under-the-radar bingo parlors throughout the United States, many of which are engaged in less-than-reputable machinations.

TWO'S COMPANY, THREE'S A CROWD

While Prague was my preferred city for various reasons, London was by far the preference of the Russian oligarchs. It would only be a matter of time before Boris or Valery latch on to a client seeking refuge for his money in London.

Several weeks had passed, and the Ruskov affair had taken on a life of its own in Moscow. Yelstin was extended Parliamentary immunity from prosecution, as were many in his family. Any further investigation of Yelstin would likely implicate Putin in corruption on a grander scale. Scapegoats were gently sanctioned, and investigations vanished or vanquished into the sunset.

As Boris pointed out, privacy doesn't exist in Russia. The security services are privy to the most intimate details, which can have troubling consequences if left unattended. Their files are a trove of facts, innuendo, and gossip.

In many respects, democracy is the preferred jurisdiction for " investment, " with all its human and civil rights and privacy protection. It provides the oligarch safety, security, and a modicum of predictability.

When Valery contacted me to tell me that Boris and Gregori had another client interested in investing in London, it was music to my ears. I had a healthy Rolodex of contacts and sources.

Again, the optics were not necessarily pristine, but the money was good, and the due diligence was perfectly legal. Russian investors during these years were swimming in cash. Whether it was from legal or illegal sources was the task of Boris and Gregori to ascertain. Mine was to

TWO'S COMPANY, THREE'S A CROWD

ensure that the "investment" was sound and the "investors" were on the right side of the law.

Because I was now aware of Gregori's ability to comprehend and speak English—I can never forget his exquisite command of English at the train platform in Minsk—I no longer had to filter everything through Valery. I could only guess the games they would play now that Valery's translation skills are no longer needed.

"So, Gregori, who is your client?"

"Well, Marty, an art broker who searches worldwide for undervalued art . . . he is considered one of the best in Moscow. . . ."

"Gregori, you always find "one of the best,". . . . do you ever find just an average investor . . . ?

"Marty, if I did, they couldn't afford you."

He had a point. Due diligence costs money. It doesn't come cheap. The average investor usually doesn't have the money to conduct due diligence and, as a result, takes foolish risks.

"Ok, Gregori . . . outline the deal for me. . . ."

"The broker here in Moscow buys costly art for some wealthy Russians . . . they like to remain anonymous . . . you can understand why I am sure . . . most of these are cash deals . . . many reputable art dealers are reluctant to deal in cash . . . you can understand that too . . . when there is a painting that a Russian wants, he needs to know whether the dealer in London can be trusted if you know what I mean . . . we are talking about big money . . . there can be zero to no risk if you know what I mean. . . ."

Gregori was adept at advancing his proposal in English but never quite saying what he meant.

I was getting the gist of what Andrei was saying. This was when no one knew much about the value of art as a vehicle to launder money. Art dealers were immune from money laundering laws. And I was certainly not an authority in the rarified world of high-end art. Counterfeit art is pervasive. Fraud on a massive scale is endemic to this rarified world. Egos, fear of public ridicule, and the arcane politics of art-world etiquette dictate secrecy and confidentiality. Andrei needed an art dealer(s) he could trust.

The only expert in this area was a former detective with the New York City Police Department who specialized in the theft of art and its counterfeiting. I could reach out to him, but I doubt he would be receptive to my inquiry. He was not in the business of dealing with wealthy Russians, who are now labeled oligarchs.

Several former Scotland Yard detectives I was pretty friendly with might be interested in partnering with me. I would need some time. I wasn't confident that I could deliver. Art appraisal was a uniquely specialized skill. Dealers were part of a very insular, incestuous world. They knew one another and shared stories but were very proprietary. It was not my "cup of tea."

I contacted my friend Tony Pullman. Tony was a former detective in the Special Branch of Scotland Yard. He investigated everything from the Irish Republic Army to West Indian ponces to the Mafia. He knew his way around London and lived and breathed its underbelly. If anyone knew the landscape, it was Pullman.

Early in Pullman's career with Scotland Yard, I often met with him regarding trans-Atlantic crime and criminals. Pullman had an encyclopedic knowledge of London's underworld. One evening, while dining in Oxfordshire, Tony observed two young boys filling a canister with gasoline. They were making a Molotov cocktail and readying it for our restaurant. Tony took flight, and I followed him. We ultimately corralled the two boys and alerted the local constabulary. It was my initial foray into London's crime scene.

I flew to London to meet Tony. We met in the West End of London. These were the neighborhoods Tony knew best from his days at the Yard. After all the routine pleasantries, I ran the opportunity past him. As I suspected, he wanted nothing to do with it. He was a die-hard Anglican who had no love for the Russians, especially their massive influx of money in London's real estate market.

He did, however, raise the possibility of partnering with him on due diligence he had involving a wealthy aristocrat. His client needed due diligence in Moscow. The client was in the hospitality business and was invited to join a consortium intending to purchase an existing hotel or build one in Moscow.

The client was skeptical about dealing in Moscow but saw the great opportunity to get in on the ground floor. Risk mitigation was all that this client was looking for. Nothing ventured, nothing gained drove his search for new opportunities.

My problem was trusting Gregori and Boris. Their credibility was certainly suspect. They will fly with the highest bidder. However, there was an option that could be helpful.

Marisha, in Prague, was connected as well, if not better, than Boris or Gregori. She had access to the moneyed class. I could use Marisha, Gregori, and Boris to play what I learned from one against the other. It would serve two purposes for me.

I could bring Matteo and Marisha into the project and learn just how duplicitous Boris and Gregori were. It was my turn to engage in counter-intelligence.

"Let's do it, Tony. Sounds like it will be fun . . . I have the sources in Moscow to get a decent read for your client." Tony was on board. He would meet with his client and work out the details. I suggested a retainer of 10,000 euros.

I contacted Gregori and told him I was unlikely to deliver for him on his art project. The risks are too high for the meager return we will earn.

He seemed disappointed. He realized his origination fee had just evaporated.

He and Boris liked the origination fee idea. They didn't have to do the "grunt work." They just had to sell the product. "Sweat equity" was their contribution.

Boris and Gregori chose to work smart.

"But Gregori, I have a client in London who needs due diligence in Moscow . . . are you interested?"

Gregori jumped at the opportunity.

"What is your hourly rate, Gregori?"

"How's two hundred U.S. dollars an hour," Marty?

In Moscow, $100 an hour was considered "good money." This wasn't London or New York. Moscow was still recovering from a self-inflicted recession.

"Gregori, it's $100 an hour . . . no more . . . the budget doesn't allow for more than that. . . ."

Of course, it didn't matter what his hourly rate was. He would fudge the hours spent on the due diligence. "We pretend to work, and you pretend to pay us" was not about to be replaced with the Western work ethic. One way or the other, the client would get screwed.

Marisha and Matteo were my aces in the hole. I knew I could depend on them to deliver, especially Marisha. Her life changed for the better. Marisha was loyal to a fault.

I suggested they fly to London and meet with Tony and me. I wanted Tony to be comfortable with Marisha and Matteo. Plus, I looked forward to spending time with them. A weekend was sufficient. Many memories; most were good.

They agreed. The following Friday, they arrived at Heathrow. I had a car service collect them and bring them to the Claridge—my favorite hotel in London. I reserved them a room for two nights. I was staying with Tony at his flat. But for convenience, Tony and I shared a room at the Claridge.

The chemistry gelled. Everybody got along and seemed to enjoy telling "war stories." I wasn't sure how Tony and Marisha would hit it off. Tony being the consummate gentleman, showed no ill will toward Marisha. If for no other reason, he recognized Marisha was our meal ticket with his client.

The financials and logistics of conducting due diligence were worked out. Marisha would take the lead. It only made sense. No one other than she could access the sources we would need to make this work. The fly in the ointment was Andrei. How would we compensate him?

Tony would be reluctant to partner with Gregori or Boris. His distaste for Russians was palpable. Meeting Gregori and Boris would only make matters worse. I could scale it back so that only Gregori would be paid. Matteo would have to agree to forego any compensation. This could work.

I would have to discuss this with Matteo separately. This would likely be my last due diligence with the Moscow and Belarussian partners. Trust had evaporated entirely. Marisha's take on Boris was spot on.

Matteo and I met the following day without Marisha or Tony. I discussed my dilemma. Again, Matteo was non-pulsed. He indicated that with Marisha taking the lead on the due diligence, "I'm sure it will all work out," suggesting that he and Marisha would reconcile their end of the budget.

Tony discussed the scope of the due diligence and the expected deliverables. His client needed to know everything about a Moscow-based group, Eurokral. This group comprised three businesspeople, one from Moscow, one from Latvia, and the other from Ukraine. The project required all of Marisha's human assets in the three countries and those of Andrei and Boris. The retainer of 10,000 euros would likely be doubled or tripled, depending on the difficulty of the assignment.

Fortunately, KGB assets in these three jurisdictions remained active. The difficulty was that Marisha, Boris, and Gregori could be tapping the same assets, which would cause Boris and Gregori become suspicious of my motives. Somehow, Marisha had to have a "cut-out," someone other than herself. She would have to plumb deep into her network of KGB assets. Trust was essential. Her fingerprints could not be on the cut-out(s).

I suggested that Marisha begin her work before I conferred with Gregori. The deliverable was relatively straightforward: do the principals have the political and financial capital to initiate and complete the proposed hotel? Determining who they were "connected with" and how they acquired their money for the joint venture would be critical.

Of course, the origins of the money would always be suspect. It was Russia where money grew on trees—especially in the 90s.

Marisha was more than raring to go. We all went to dinner on Saturday night. It was to be total immersion in London's ambiance. No shop talk. Just pure enjoyment. The weeks ahead would be enough time to engage in the intricacies of due diligence. This was their time to embellish their credibility with Tony.

Naturally, I was concerned about Marisha's and Matteo's affinity for imbibing to the point of intoxication. I could not afford any unprofessional behavior in Tony's presence. Either I had to see that Tony had an early evening in the city, or Marisha and Matteo had to finish the evening in the privacy of their well-appointed room. Tony was a stickler when it came to the appropriate etiquette.

Fortunately, after Tony had dinner with us, he excused himself. I suspect he knew we wanted to enjoy a night or two in London. To Tony, this was home, and he took what we loved about London for granted. Next to New York, it is Europe's playground for the rich and infamous.

I suggested we go to Maxim's, a private casino in South Kensington. London's laws on gambling were rather strict, requiring patrons to register before being admitted to a casino. Their casinos were understated and tastefully blended into the community. This was not Las Vegas, Atlantic City, or Prague. Gaming was a necessary evil that was neither promoted nor prohibited. It was tolerated.

Maxim's casino host was a valuable, long-term friend of mine. Joan Summers, whose significant other was a former Scotland Yard detective, welcomed us to the casino, pulling out all stops to impress Matteo and Marisha.

For Marisha, this was a special treat. She had never been to London and was fascinated by the wealth of the clientele. She relished the rich mahogany décor, mood lighting, and diverse client base. Middle Easterners, gambling away their oil riches, a smattering of Russians, and a few Chinese made it an ethnic kaleidoscope. Marisha was mesmerized by the subtle and muted electricity that permeated the atmosphere.

It was as if Baz Luhrmann had created a movie set for a *Great Gatsby* filming. Everybody dressed to the tens, with their better jewelry sparkling as if it was professionally polished.

Joan had arranged a separate enclave for us to sit and people watch. Marisha was intent on joining in at the tables and gambling a bit. I emphasized that you never win in a casino; the house always wins.

"Marisha, let me explain it to you with another simple idiom. There is only one way to win in a casino. Own it."

Marisha and Matteo both laughed. Matteo gave Marisha a couple of hundred euros to play with. The rule was simple. If you win, you buy us dinner tomorrow night. And if you lose, you buy us dinner tomorrow night.

"That's a stupid rule, Marty . . . I lose either way. . . ."

"I think it's Matteo who loses . . . but you actually will win . . . you will have learned an invaluable lesson . . . the house always wins . . . look around . . . it's not free what you see . . . someone or many bodies pay for this opulence and exclusivity . . . all those people at the tables . . . but enjoy yourself . . . it's your night out. . . ."

As Marisha gambled away Matteo's money, it gave me a chance to speak with Matteo. I was interested in how Marisha was acclimating to work. Matteo could not be happier.

"She has a great work ethic Marty . . . and she's fun to have around . . . everything is so new to her that she asks funny questions, which is okay with me . . . it forces me to think about what I've taken for granted. . . ."

"How's she doing with Guisippina . . . is there any female rivalry, especially with your relationship with Marisha. . . ."

"Guisippina wasn't happy when she found out we were living together . . . she felt like Marisha would start thinking she was in charge . . . I let Marisha know in no uncertain terms that Guisippina is special, and she was not to antagonize or order her around . . . I think Marisha gets it. . . ."

"As for Gusipinnna, she's quite mature and isn't intimidated by Marisha . . . I think it will be okay, but what's that saying, "two's company, three's a crowd . . . time will tell. . . ."

"Matteo, where'd you get that idiom, two's company, three's a crowd?"

"From Marisha . . . ".

I was not too fond of Matteo's answer. To me, it was an ominous sign of what was to come.

We had a couple of drinks and returned to the Claridge. Marisha, as expected, lost her, or should I say Matteo's, money. Dinner was on Marisha, regardless.

Tony was soundly asleep when I entered the room. I quietly undressed, brushed my teeth, gargled, and went to bed. It was a telling evening that left me a bit uneasy. Boris's words—you can't mix work with pleasure—reverberated in my head. The Guisippina-Marisha situation was troubling. And I blame myself.

Marisha and Matteo would be leaving later in the day. We met for brunch, discussed last-minute details, reflected on Marisha's budding experience in a British casino, and saw Matteo and Marisha off.

Tony and I returned to his flat and watched good old-fashion football—soccer.

LONDONSTAD—AN OLIGARCH'S NIRVANA

In discussions with Tony, his obsession with the Russian money pouring into London was enlightening on one hand but disturbing on another. He was angry that this money was making its way into the campaigns of British politicians. He lamented how British politics are looking more and more like politics in America.

He witnessed entire neighborhoods slowly gobbled up by outlandish sums of money, making housing virtually unaffordable to the average middle-class Londoner. It was not the London he grew up in or one he wanted his children and grandchildren to experience.

He suggested we take a taxi to Eatonsquare, where the Russians buy real estate as if it were a fire sale.

"Marty, my colleagues at The Yard, are telling me that nobody knows who owns these properties . . . deeds do not reflect the ownership . . . all are cash buyers . . . it's terrible what's happening to this great country. . . ."

Age can impose a nostalgic slant on much of what we think and say. The so-called "good-ole-days" weren't as good as we remember them. There was much to regret. Colonization, the slave trade, racism, xenophobia, and homophobia are at the top. But perhaps the simplicity we brought to growing up in another era makes the changes Tony was experiencing seem chaotic.

"Tony, I'm sure our parents saw rock-n-roll, the Beatles, and the Stones as the death knell of innocence . . . every generation looks at the next and questions 'how'd we get it so wrong?'. . . . if you don't change with the times, you go the way of the dinosaur . . . think of how much better your life has been than that of your parents. . . ."

"But will my children's and grandchildren's life be better, Marty . . . that's my fear?"

"Tony, we had our crack at it; it's their turn now . . . this world either breaks you or makes you. . . . as the saying goes, what doesn't break you, only makes you stronger . . . we ran the gauntlet, and we're still in the mix . . . not a bad run for two old private eyes. . . ."

As we reflected on our lives, Tony continued to obsess over the incursion of the Russian oligarchs. He was assembling dossiers on those his sources had identified as owning property in London.

Naturally, I was interested in what Tony had to say. London was the favorite destination of an emerging class of Russian oligarchs. London was open for the pickings with its robust and accessible financial markets and the lack of credible money-laundering controls. Undoubtedly, I would spend time in London and Prague as I delved into this relatively new and exciting investigative endeavor.

Throughout the week, Tony and I would visit different parts of England. Surrey, Brighton, Norfolk, and a little village called Blackboys— named for the coal mining industry that once was the only employer there—were some of Tony's favorite haunts. They brought him back to his younger years growing up in Cambridge. And they allowed him to escape the torturous chaos that London now represented.

Upon our return from Norfolk, we received a call from Marisha. She could enlist a "cut-out" in Moscow who understood the need for maximum opacity. There could be no connection between the cut-out and Marisha.

Tony and I met with his client, Maximilian "Max" Powis, in London. Powis was the real deal. He had significant real estate investments in London. Hotels and commercial complexes were his forte.' Powis explained his reluctance to partner with Russians. He knew the landscape in Moscow was one of duplicity, bribery, and outright thievery. Without a *roof*, business would likely result in a poison pill, an unfortunate accident, or a bullet in the head. It was not a welcoming investment environment.

With that said, for those who invested early, Russia was the answer to the great gold rush that put California on the radar of the adventurous prospector. "Nothing ventured, nothing gained" made millionaires out of paupers. All Powis wanted was risk mitigation. We offered him that insurance.

Powis had the names of three investors he was considering in a joint venture. There was Dimitri Rockoff, Ivan Kostingan, and Daniel Dimostrovski. They all lived in Moscow but would frequent London regularly. Max was unaware of any real estate holdings they may have in London, although "you never know with Russians . . . do they ever tell you the whole truth? . . . ," the added touch to most of his sentences.

His concern was two-fold: do they have the financial means to engage in multi-million dollar hotel and commercial projects, and are they well insinuated with the political players in Moscow? Powis understood that these were unpredictable times. Political alliances were fluid and transitory. Your *roof* today is your competitor's muscle tomorrow. The highest bidder is equated with loyalty.

I contacted Marisha and provided her with the three names. Rockoff was in Moscow, Kostigan in Latvia, and Dimostrovski in Ukraine. They were part of a cobbled-together consortium that would look for investment opportunities in these three countries. Fortunately, her cut-out had assets in all three countries. It was apparent that the cut-out would be tapping into KGB. Marisha was not about to share her cut-out with me. Marisha learned quickly!

I reached out to Gregori and provided him with the names. I played coy with Gregori, giving him only one name and assessing whether what he uncovered was consistent with what I had learned from Marisha. In this way, if I felt that Gregori was less than honest, he would not know of the other two investors and possibly sabotage any investment opportunity for the client.

I gave him Dimitri Rockoff since he was in Moscow. I told Gregori that the other two persons were in Latvia and Ukraine, and I would outsource those to my other assets. Gregori was not happy. He saw his billable hours whittled down. I knew that would be an issue, but I lost all trust in Gregori and Boris. But I didn't need enemies in Moscow, so I told Andrei that he would be handsomely compensated and didn't have to work hard. That was music to Gregori's ears.

As expected, Marisha delivered. Rockoff was the son of Simon Rockoff, who had exclusive rights to mineral mining in Siberia. His wealth, at the time, was in the hundreds of millions. Rockoff would use his son to scout investment opportunities, primarily Western investors.

According to Marisha, "being involved with Rockoff was like sitting in the Kremlin . . . He took care of Yelstin and his cronies . . . he has the money and connections to make it work . . . I can't say it would be a risky investment for your client . . . but like anything in Moscow now, that could change tomorrow. . . ."

I was waiting to get a read-out from Gregori. Days would pass, and nothing. I called Gregori, and no one answered the phone. Several days of calling passed, and I contacted Valery.

"Valery, it's Marty. . . ."

"Like I didn't know . . . how could I mistake that New York accent. . . ." Valery responded.

"Have you heard from Gregori? . . . he seems to have disappeared . . . he's gone dark on me, Valery."

"Let me see if I can reach him . . . if not, I'll reach out to Boris. . . ."

Valery then asked about Marisha and how she was doing in Prague. Marisha was a fixation for the Moscow/Belarus group. They were envious of her cunning skill in insinuating herself into the Western lifestyle.

"She seems to be doing just fine, Valery . . . I'll send her your regards . . . Boris's as well," getting a subtle dig in.

"Do that, Marty . . . hopefully we'll get to Prague or London soon?"

Little did Valery know, but his partnership with me was over. I could tell from speaking with him that he was unaware of Gregori's due diligence assignment. Doing business in Russia seldom ends up well. Someone or somebodies always walks away dissatisfied, angry, or looking for revenge. It's not a pretty picture; at least it wasn't in the 90s.

After speaking with Valery, I contacted Marisha, hoping she could enlighten me regarding Andrei's disappearance. She had heard nothing, which was unusual. Marisha had her ear against the ground in Moscow, even when she wasn't there. She said she would reach out to her assets and find out what she could.

Within hours, she called me back.

"Marty, Gregori is dead . . . they found him with his fingers cut off and rubles stuck up his ass. . . ."

"You gotta be joking, Marisha."

"Nope, he was playing with the big boys . . . they don't like liars and cheats . . . By the way, he was killed . . . sounds like he was greedy . . . he had his hand in too many pockets. . . ."

I thought that lying and cheating were par for the course in Russia. Guess it's the old story. Gregori got caught.

"Marisha, here's another idiom for you "It's all about whose ox is being gored," Gregori upset the wrong people . . . it's an old Judaic saying. . . ."

"Marty, I can write a book on American idioms if I learn nothing else from you."

"Marisha, with that and two dollars, you can get a cup of coffee . . . another idiom for you. . . ."

One less irritation to deal with. And I have to believe Valery knew and chose not to tell me. Messages sent in this manner are for a reason. Valery, Boris, and Andrei did not share in the spoils. Gregori apparently paid the price. Perhaps he was the greediest.

It reminded me of another idiom to tell Marisha; "pigs get fed, hogs get slaughtered."

This was Russia 1990s. You never knew who was with you and who was after you. It was a roll of the dice, and as Andrei found out, snake eyes can be fatal.

For me, the good part was they were out of the picture. I had Marisha, and that's all I needed. It made it much easier for me. My head was bursting with clever machinations that kept me awake at night. One KGB was enough. Four was a calamity.

THERE'S AN EXPEDITER
IN EVERY CITY

With Marisha, there was little she couldn't accomplish over the telephone. She knew who to call and what they could deliver. Her human assets from her years in KGB and her family provided her entre' to the more rarified levers of power in Moscow and throughout the former Soviet Union. She knew what buttons to push.

When Marisha told me she had to go to Riga and Kyiv, I wasn't sure the budget could cover the costs. I quizzed her on why she had to travel there.

"Marty, sometimes meeting face to face can tell me more than a phone call. We have to get this right for your client, don't we?"

I contacted Tony, who agreed. He was not concerned with the budget. Max would underwrite the costs knowing he was getting an accurate read on his prospective partners.

I advised Marisha to go and keep me informed on the progress.

Marisha arrived first in Riga. There she met with her contacts. After all the usual pleasantries, Marisha got down to business.

She needed to know everything she could about Ivan Kostigan and his relationship with Dimitri Rockoff, Moscow, and Daniel Dimostrovsky, Kyiv. Financial assets, relationships with government officials, and connections to the underworld.

Kostigan was a respected businessman in Riga. He had financial interests in several commercial projects. He sat on the board of Riga International Import and Export Bank. His financial pedigree appeared solid.

The bank likely laundered money for shady and unscrupulous businessmen and gangsters. Without any substantive evidence, it was a risk factor that had to be considered but was unlikely to be dispositive.

Regarding construction in Riga, it was no different than in Moscow. There's a people like Rockoff, Kostigan, and Dimostrovsky in every city worldwide. They *expedite* that which would take months and years to wind through unwieldy and corrupt bureaucracies. Without "connections" in government, permits were delayed or disapproved, construction projects were slapped with "stop work" orders, and contractors were reluctant to do the work without guarantees. Kostigan either paid off or struck out.

Additionally, it was likely that the local underworld was getting its share of any construction project. Riga's underbelly was no different than found in Moscow and Kyiv. "Tribute" or "kickbacks" to those criminal groups controlling territory was part of business costs.

Kostigan, Rockoff, and Dimostrovsky attended Moscow's prestigious Bauman Technical University, all three receiving their PhDs there. Venturing out independently, each gravitated to the countries they were born or raised in. They remained in contact over the decades, and when this project in Moscow "got legs," they formed a consortium and sought investors from the West. Nothing seemed to preclude Powis from partnering with them.

Marisha then went to Kyiv. There the landscape was riddled with corruption at every level of government—from the traffic cop on the street to the President and his circle of cronies. The bureaucracy was stifling.

While Dimostrovsky was a successful developer in Kyiv, his success was rooted in his connections in the upper political world which gangsters and racketeers dominated. It was his only option. There was little doubt that Dimostrovsky had the "street smarts" to navigate Moscow's treacherous political infrastructure.

Marisha returned to Prague via London. She met with Tony and me to discuss what she had uncovered. Tony was a bit standoffish, mostly listening but saying little. I could tell from Tony's body language that he lacked trust in Marisha.

Marisha was booked at the Claridge for the night. I could tell that this might get complicated. As much as I distanced myself from Marisha, she would pull me back.

"Marty, can your friend Joan get us into Maxim's tonight? . . . I'd love to have dinner there."

"Let me see what I can arrange, Marisha."

Joan was more than accommodating. She arranged for us to have dinner, absent Tony, who had no interest in joining us.

Over dinner, Marisha and I discussed her situation in Prague with Matteo. She was guarded and said virtually nothing about office politics. Of course, you learn that saying nothing is an asset or commodity in this business. And to the contrary, what is not said says more than what is.

Marisha was interested in how my life was progressing.

"Does the unassailable mistress still order you around?" Marisha asked.

"Of course, Marisha . . . it's what got you the trip to Riga and Kyiv . . . and Prague as well. . . ."

Marisha wanted to try her hand at the tables again. I warned her, "Marisha, who is it that only wins in a casino?"

"I know, Marty, the owners . . . but I enjoy it . . . just a couple of hands . . . then we'll leave. . . ."

Marisha played a couple of hands and lost whatever she gambled.

I got Marisha a taxi back to the Claridge and kissed her good night. I told her a car service would collect her and take her to the airport the following day.

"Marisha, be ready by 10 A.M. . . . the car service will be here by then. . . ."

"Marty, why don't you wake me so you're sure I'm ready . . . ?

"I don't think that would be a good idea, Marisha."

She knew that I would never take her up on it. Matteo was too good a friend.

Of course, Marisha was another story. Her flirtatious ways could get her into trouble. And may have on prior occasions?

Now that we have the "skinny" on Dimitri, Ivan, and Daniel, we could meet with Max and discuss his options. Ultimately, it was his decision whether to pursue this investment opportunity. All we could do was suggest how to mitigate risk.

MOSCOW: A DIAMOND IN THE VERY ROUGH

Unlike New York City, which is essentially a concrete jungle, Moscow is a city that relishes its parks and rivers. Notwithstanding its horrid weather, its beauty lies in the Mongolian architecture that adorns the center city, from St. Basil's Cathedral to the Kremlin.

But underneath the polished veneer lies a wretched underbelly. Unless you enter this cruel and unforgiving world, you can't fathom the paranoia that tracks your every move.

As one who has enjoyed America's freedoms, a prison mentality best describes how you navigate your life in Moscow. From the point of view of an outsider, it seems that when you grow up under these grim and dreadful conditions, you adapt to the endless abuses a totalitarian regime inflicts on its people over time. You become numb to the routine injustices and provocations. Perhaps it is no different than being intellectually stymied by the accouterments afflicting children of privilege.

Tony and I now had to explain to Max the risks he might encounter as he entered a new world. This was not for the faint-hearted. It took courage, fortitude, and money to withstand the onslaught of problems he was about to confront. Doing business in Moscow requires nerves of steel.

I should have never underestimated Max's gentile British sensibilities.

"Marty, did you forget what country survived the Blitzkrieg, Dunkirk, and went on to win the war? Don't misconstrue British civility for weakness. . . . never assume that people born of privilege lack grit. . . ."

Max understood what he was about to get into.

"Marty, you know we need some sponsor there . . . Are Dimitri, Daniel, and Ivan connected enough that they will be able to run interference?"

"Max, I intend to go through that with you."

Tony and I discussed Max's partners and what they brought to the consortium. We discussed the likelihood that he would have to retain at least one "expediter," or maybe two or three. It all depended on what Dimitri Rockoff, the Moscow representative, was able to arrange through his connections.

Rockoff was the key to making this commercial venture in Moscow work. He had the "connections," the money, and entre to the construction trades. Of course, relying solely on Rockoff's assets led to the familiar warning, "never put all our eggs in one basket." Max was doing just that.

FOUR'S COMPANY

When I began in this business, I was under the mistaken belief that conducting due diligence for prospective investors was a relatively honest and worthwhile endeavor. What doesn't an investor want to know about whom he is joining up with? It's a relatively benign inquiry that demands "only the facts." Once presented with "the facts," the investor makes the final decision based on his experience applying risk versus benefit.

In Russia, it is not quite that simple. Because every financial arrangement involves any number of people taking their cut or "stepping on it," the ultimate cost to the investor could skyrocket.

A recent example was the construction costs associated with the 2014 Winter Olympics. According to news reports, two of Putin's oligarchs, the largest Russian gas company and Russia's largest bank, demanded an additional billion dollars in cost overruns. The project alone cost fifty billion dollars—the most significant expenditure on any Olympic endeavor. How much of this involved bribery, money laundering, and outright thievery, is anybody's guess? This was Putin's signature project that would "put lipstick on a pig," for want of a better metaphor. Or, more appropriately, on a hog before being slaughtered.

This is what Max, under the Yelstin regime, faced long before Sochi and Putin ascended.

Under Yeltsin, *blat* (i.e., informal agreements, connections, black market deals) was not as rigorous or systematic. Under Putin, *blat* became institutionalized and indistinguishable from Russia's "civil" society.

Max understood the implications of partnering with Eurokral. Wisely, he leveraged Dimitri, Ivan, and Daniel's relationship with the banks in Moscow, Latvia, and Kyiv to compensate for his anticipated losses.

Max understood that the personal piggy banks of Euokral and his three Soviet partners would be first in line to take the bulk of losses—which were inevitable. Max did not intend to "be on the hook." Nor did his investors.

With financing in place, construction was about to begin.

Max decided to go to Moscow and meet with Dimitri, Ivan, and Daniel. They could all speak or understand English, with Ivan having a better command of the language. I could send Marisha with Max, but unconvinced, that would be wise. Marisha could be a bit unmanageable, and she might cross paths with Boris. Knowing Boris, he probably knew about Max through Gregori and was waiting to sink his claws into him. Marisha would be counter-productive if that were to occur.

I decided to have Marisha arrange a meeting in London between her cut-out, Max, Tony, and me. Marisha should be at this meeting to make the appropriate introductions and lay the ground rules.

I contacted Matteo and asked if I could borrow Marisha for a couple of days. There would be a sizable stipend in it for both Marisha and him. He had no problem with Marisha coming to London but suggested he tag along. Of course, that was a no-brainer.

The following week, Marisha, Olga (i.e., Marisha's cutout), Max, Tony, and Matteo would meet in the conference room at the Claridge. We discussed the lay of the land with Max, with Olga taking the lead. Olga spoke fluent English and several other languages. There was little doubt that Olga was a "former" KGB. My concern was about Boris and whether Olga and Boris were connected previously or now.

I wasted no time. "Olga, I need to know whether you know Boris?" She assured me that there was no relationship.

"My contacts are a lot higher than Boris . . . There won't be any spillage. . . ."

I was unsure how she knew Boris's ranking in KGB's hierarchy. I assumed that Marisha had told her about Boris. It was a nagging *faux pas*.

Olga would be introduced as Max's project manager in Moscow. She would oversee all administrative issues with budgeting, contracts, and personnel. Max would check with Olga daily, receive progress reports, and discuss any problems that may develop on the job site or among the consortium.

Max would leave for Moscow the following week, meet with Olga, and arrange to meet with the consortium partners. As the meeting was about to end, I suggested we go for dinner at Maxim's. Max had other plans.

He suggested we join him at his favorite Italian restaurant, Quaglino's. Max was an oenophile who loved the wines of Piedmonte. Barolo's were his favorite, but Barbaresco was, "according to Max," the most underval-ued wine among the Piedmonte aristocrats.

Interesting, I thought. I would get an education on Italian wines from Max, an Englishman.

We freshened up, and off to Quaglino's, we taxied. Tony was on board, knowing that Max would find it impolite had Tony not joined us for dinner.

Marisha was again impressed with the ambiance and the fine wines that Max was ordering. It was apparent that the Western lifestyle was of Marisha's choosing.

Also, Olga seemed to enjoy chatting it up with Max. I suspected that Olga envisioned a life in London and Moscow, savoring the more refined things Max seemed to enjoy.

Marisha, Matteo, and I were chatting it up, with Tony looking bored and out of his element. I suspect Marisha and Olga realized that Moscow and Russia were not to Tony's taste. There was no chemistry between them.

Marisha suggested we all go to Maxims after dinner. Tony was unin-terested. Max, Olga, Matteo, Marisha, and I were in. I called Joan, and she invited us to join her and her beau, John, for after-dinner drinks.

The night at Maxim's was the typical crowd—Middle Easterners, Russians, and Chinese. Of course, Marisha had to donate to Maxims Charity Fund. Olga just watched. Max played several hands and won. He had the money to outlast the house. Marisha did not!

The night was getting on. I excused myself. Max, Olga, Matteo, and Marisha eventually all left together. I asked no questions. It was none of my business.

When I arrived at Tony's flat, he was still awake. I could see he was bothered.

"Marty, I'm concerned about Olga . . . I'm not sure she's the right fit for Max. . . ."

"Max is three times seven, Tony . . . he can handle himself . . . I'll have Marisha talk to Olga and strongly tell Olga that it has to be a business relationship and nothing more. . . ."

"Yeah, I'm sure Marisha gets it . . . look at her and Matteo . . . don't you get it, Marty? These Russian women are all looking for a way to get out of that shit-hole . . . Olga sees Max as her ticket out. . . ."

"Well, Tony, let me make it simple . . . we pull the plug on this due diligence, or ride the bronco until it drops dead . . . welcome to Moscow on the Thames . . . it's a new world . . . read the papers . . . globalization is the future. . . ."

"Marty, I'm not sure I'm made for this merry-go-round. . . ."

"Neither am I, but we're on it, and if we jump off now, we'll get hurt, and so will Max. . . . let's get some sleep . . . tomorrow is always brighter. . . ."

EYES WIDE SHUT

The following day, Tony and I shower, have breakfast, and call Max at his home. There was no answer. I then reach out to Matteo at the Claridge. Again no response. They disappeared, neither accepting phone calls. I told Tony in time that Max or Matteo would find us. Tony was less than happy about the situation. He saw trouble ahead.

Later in the day, I get a call at Tony's flat. Its Matteo.

"Matteo, where have you been . . . I've tried to reach you and Max all day, and no answer . . . Is Max okay?"

"Relax, Marty, we're all okay . . . we had a night in the city and slept in . . . Olga's with Max . . . they went to Max's house in Kensington . . . I'm sure if you call him now, he'll answer. . . ."

I told Tony to reach out to Max. Max finally answered the phone. He never mentioned that Olga was with him, but it didn't matter. We knew. I decided to sit down with Max upon Olga's return to Moscow and discuss the unacceptable risk thresholds he should consider. Whether he had crossed the Rubicon already, I felt it was only appropriate to discuss the typical *modus operendi* of KGB.

Olga was departing the following day, returning to Moscow. A meeting would be arranged in Moscow between Max and his consortium partners. Olga would be introduced as his project manager in Moscow. Tony and I decided to remove ourselves from the foursome. There was no need to interfere in what had become a lovefest.

The following day, Olga, Marisha, and Matteo leave London. Olga to Moscow, Matteo, and Marisha to Prague. We arrange to meet Max and discuss the red lines he should avoid while in Moscow.

"Max, Tony, and I think it's only appropriate to discuss the temptations you will face in Moscow . . . the obvious one is the prostitutes that your partners will make available to you . . . being single, it's unlikely they will use this for extorting you, but you should remain vigilant that you are not set up for a false charge of sexual assault or rape . . . always remember that no matter where you stay, you are likely being surveilled on camera . . . there are no zones of privacy in Moscow . . . your every move is captured either on camera or through physical or audio surveillance. . . ."

"I understand, Marty . . . I intend to use Olga as my beard . . . that may avoid these uncomfortable situations. . . ."

"Max, that brings me to Olga . . . I am not interested in your current relationship with Olga . . . understand she is KGB . . . there are no former KGB . . . they live and breathe that life . . . she knows your finances . . . and how you live here in London . . . you are a catch . . . or should I say a mark . . . she will ingratiate herself to you . . . while you may think you are in control now, she will reverse the tables . . . I know you think I'm overdramatic or even cynical . . . I have to warn you . . . be careful . . .

"Marty, I wasn't born yesterday . . . I'm fully aware of Olga's motives and in control of the situation . . . let's leave it at that. . . ."

I could see that Max would have none of it. He had his mind made up and was confident he could weather anything. We had no idea what the future held. That slippery slope was about to be greased.

DUPLICITY

If you learn nothing else when dealing with the Moscow mafia, what you see is not what you get. There are side deals behind every business arrangement—usually more than one. Everybody in the food chain has their hand out. When you think you have solved one problem, another pops up. It's the nature of the beast, or should I say bear?

And if you think the police or MVD are your friends, think twice. They, too, have their hand out, looking for someone to "wet the beak." As an outsider, you are essentially naked. You have no protection other than the goodwill of your *roofs* which are in it for the money.

Under Yelstin, these alliances changed continuously. A favorite expression was "whack the mole." You take care of one "expediter," and another appears. It was endless under Yelstin. There are expediters in all cities worldwide, but Moscow's expediters are the *crème-de le-crème*.

We educated Max about this, but Max knew he could navigate this treacherous maze of fleeting relationships. Hubris is the ultimate Achilles heel that falls many business executives.

All Tony could see were problems. If he had his way, he would extricate himself from this arrangement. Max was headed for disaster. There was nothing we could do to dissuade Max from pursuing this investment opportunity. In Max's eyes, the return on investment was too good to be true. And usually, it is.

When Max arrived in Moscow, Olga was there to greet him. She had taken care of lodging arrangements, planned the business meeting, accompanied him to the anticipated construction site, met with the architects and engineers, and sat down with his partners from Eurokral.

Olga's efficiency and work ethic made her indispensable to Max. That's just like she liked it, and that's how Max was slowly drawn into Olga's lair. Except there was no way out without Olga.

No doubt, Olga and Max had more than a business relationship. Max was infatuated or seduced by Olga's charm, beauty, and knowledge. He was dealing with someone who had mastered her craft. She was exceptionally skillful in the art of counterintelligence.

Periodically, I would reach out to Marisha to get a read on Olga and Max. Seldom would Marisha get anything of value, simply telling me that Max is doing fine. "Olga is taking good care of him," Marisha would say.

"I'm sure, Marisha . . . that's what I'm concerned about."

"You're so cynical, Marty . . . can't you just accept that Olga has Max's best interests at heart? . . . remember she was my cut-out when you needed information on Daniel, Ivan, and Dimitri . . . she delivered . . . you were satisfied. . . ."

I wasted my time with Marisha, and Tony wasted his time with Max. We were essentially ghosted—out of the loop. Other than personally traveling to Moscow, which I had no intention of doing, Max was on his own —naked in Moscow.

As time passed and Tony and I learned less and less from Marisha and Max, our only option was to have Marisha reach out to Boris and try getting a read on Max, Eurokral, and the partners. That was dangerous, given their contentious relationship. Oleg was the only option I had left.

I contacted Matteo and asked that he not discuss our conversation with Marisha. Another risk, I thought. I told Matteo of my concerns regarding Max, Olga, and the consortium.

"Matteo, do you think we could use Oleg to dig up anything on Max and the Moscow consortium without Marisha's knowledge? I am at a loss over what to do. It's billable and non-negotiable. Whatever the costs, we will pay. . . ."

I knew Tony could convince Max to cover the expenditures. Max wasn't stingy, although he could be frugal over the silliest things. He had a penchant for cigars but would only buy the cheapest ones. His favorite line was, "I hate to see my money go up in smoke."

Matteo had Oleg contact me. Oleg suggested he come to London so that we could give him a thorough briefing.

"No problem, Oleg . . . give us the date and the time of your arrival . . . we'll have you collected at Heathrow. . . ."

Within two days, Oleg arrived. Tony and I gave him a briefing. We discussed Max and his relationship with Olga. We shared with him our due diligence on Daniel, Ivan, Dimitri, and Eurokral.

When we brought up Eurokral, Oleg reacted, and not favorably. He knew the company but did not know much about the three partners. He questioned whether our due diligence was accurate, as did Tony and I.

Oleg then blew our minds. From his knowledge, he told us that KGB created Eurokral to launder money on behalf of Yelstin and his cronies. Olga or Marisha or both likely misled us. Surprise, surprise, surprise!

Our goal was to extricate Max from what could be a likely scenario—the fall guy for any blowback that implicates Yelstin in this money-laundering enterprise. We dubbed it Operation Clorox.

Oleg was to go to Moscow and convince Max to return to London or kidnap him. We were pretty serious—kidnapping Max was not out of the question.

Oleg agreed to fly to Moscow, but kidnapping Max was out of the question. He would coax, cajole, encourage, and impress Max on why remaining in Moscow was not a "healthy" option—to use Oleg's words.

No good could come from Max's affiliation with Eurokral, Dimitri, Daniel, or Ivan. Max was playing with gasoline, a strike away from an explosion or implosion.

What was more disheartening on our end was being duped or misled by Olga or Marisha.

Why is a money-laundering scheme attached to a Russian business arrangement every time? Perhaps it is inherent in authoritarian regimes that smother and extinguish individual initiative. Likely, a combination of greed and avarice unleashes the human condition to engage in deception.

I contacted Marisha and asked her and Matteo to come to London. It was time to have an old-fashion sitdown—a heart-to-heart talk. It could not be over the phone and had to be in Matteo's presence. I suggested that Guisippina come as well, but that was a non-starter. There was no way that Marisha or Matteo would agree to that.

We met them at Tony's office when Marisha and Matteo arrived in London. I called Joan to arrange a room at Maxim's. She agreed. Later in the day, we taxied to Maxims. In the ornate conference room, tastefully furnished and well-stocked with spirits, wines, and *hor'd oeuvres*, Joan knew how to set the stage and put our guests at ease.

As we sat around this deeply-grained mahogany table, I looked Marisha in the eye and said, "Marisha, no more fucking games . . . what the fuck happened with Eurokral . . . you had to know it was KGB and a money-laundering machine? They've been laundering money from the Communist party for years . . . and you are telling me you didn't know . . . stop the bullshit. . . ."

Marisha knew I was pissed, and I was not having any more of her KGB nonsense.

Marisha was just as blunt. "Marty, had I known, why would I not have told you? . . . I knew you had other ways to find out . . . I am insulted that you think I would mislead you. . . ."

She then started to cry. Either it was a superb performance, or Marisha was genuinely offended. At this point, I gave up. Tony didn't, however.

Tears would not get in the way of Tony's anger.

"Marisha, there is no doubt that you knew more than you told us, especially about Eurokral . . . your connections in Moscow reach into the nomenklatura of the Kremlin . . . and you never knew . . . do you think I was born yesterday . . . ?

Marisha composed herself and shot back.

"Tony, I know you don't like me . . . you don't like Russians . . . you are angry, and you have a right to be . . . but do you forget, I had to use Olga as a cut-out . . . I couldn't involve myself . . . if Boris found out about my engagement, he would track it back to Marty . . . we agreed that I could not have my fingerprints on this assignment . . . I have no idea whether Olga misled you or she was in the dark . . . I don't know what to tell you . . . don't trust me then. . . ."

Matteo was visibly uncomfortable. He was taken aback by our attack on Marisha's integrity and character. Later, he told me in the privacy of the loo that he was also offended by Tony's and my demeanor.

"Marty, can I remind you of a line out of the Godfather? "Never hate your enemies. It affects your judgment. . . ." Tony's and your judgment have been affected . . . Tony lives in the past . . . he doesn't understand the new world. . . ."

There was no sense in "beating a dead horse." Ah, another idiom for Marisha, I thought.

Extracting Max from Moscow was our primary goal at this point. Whether or not Olga misled us was immaterial. If she was engaged in some counter-intelligence or clever shenanigans, there was nothing we could do about it at this point. Max's safety was our only concern. The longer he stayed and played in Moscow, the more likely trouble would follow.

MAKE MAX AN OFFER
HE CAN'T REFUSE

There is nothing harder than dealing with a successful, wealthy businessman. They only remember their triumphs and conveniently forget or ignore the mistakes along the way. Critical self-reflection is papered over with green-backs.

Success was Max's genius. Had I been half as successful as Max, I would not be a janitor cleaning up the mess he left behind.

Indeed, the number of businessmen that ultimately fell on hard times, filed for bankruptcy, committed suicide, or ended up in prison is legendary. There was no need to educate Max on the consequences of thinking with the wrong head. That conversation would go nowhere.

Brainstorming with Oleg, we decided the best approach would be one that enlisted Olga. Her influence over Max would be crucial to convincing Max to return to London, with or without Olga. We needed to get Max out of the forest so that he might see the trees. Being captive to this intriguing but unforgiving environment is intoxicating. I know. I was there. There is an attraction that is both captivating and yet frightening. It is hard to describe in words unless you experience it.

Olga was well aware of the money-laundering schemes that Eurokral was running through the banks of Moscow, Latvia, and Ukraine. There was no way she couldn't have known. Olga was conveniently blind. She was probably involved in the scams, especially with her KGB background.

Max was either clueless, in love, or involved. Two of the three were enough to know that Max would be the fall guy if exposed. Olga would escape scrutiny, as would Dimitri, Ivan, and Daniel. Max was the outsider brought inside to add the veneer of legitimacy to Eurokral. It was the perfect narrative for a Shakespearean tragedy.

With Oleg in the picture, maybe, we could extricate Max from what would happen if the scam continued. It was a long shot, but our only shot.

Oleg's relationship with Boris would prove critical. The first thing he did was contact Boris to ascertain what he knew about Eurokral and the consortium. Boris knew a lot. Andrei kept him appraised on what we were up to. Boris also knew that Olga was a shill for Max and was "playing Max" for all he was worth. And Boris also knew there was a lot of money involved, and he wanted a healthy piece of it.

Greed can be a motivating force if used wisely. This was our turn to use Max's money wisely and buy Boris. The cost was negligible. Max's freedom had no price.

Oleg, of course, had his price. Again, there was no limit to what we would pay to get Max out of this self-induced stupor.

"Oleg, let's not talk about what this will cost now; what's your plan?"

"We could kidnap him, Marty," Oleg said sarcastically. "We'll put him on the next flight to London drugged up. . . ."

"Oleg, knock it off . . . enough of your spy nonsense. . . ."

"Okay, Marty, this is the plan . . . Olga will beg Max to take her to Monaco . . . she had always wanted to go to the casino there and hob-knob with the rich and famous . . . Max loves to gamble, as you know . . . I can't see him saying no to Olga . . . once we get him to Monaco, Tony and you fly in and insist he returns to London, that a serious matter involving his investment in Eurokral has come up . . . and he must meet with the people in London who are inquiring . . . in the event, he refuses, drug him, put him on the plane as if he were drunk . . . and get out of Monaco . . . He's your problem when he gets to London. . . ."

"That's brilliant, Oleg."

"That's why you pay me big money, Marty."

I knew this wasn't going to be cheap. We were going to pay and pay dearly. Or should I say Max would pay dearly?

"So, Oleg, what's the budget for this?

"How's $200,000, Marty?"

I was taken aback. I would have thought the sky was the limit.

"No problem, Oleg . . . where does Boris fit into this . . . ?"

"That's for me to worry about, not you, Marty."

I later discovered that Olga took Marisha's place in Boris's life. Boris was a serial philanderer despite his training and philosophical musings about work and pleasure not mixing. Olga would do whatever Boris told her. The money was divided equally—$100,000 for Oleg and $100,000 for Boris and his lover, Olga.

Of course, that's above the costs associated with their time in Monaco.

"Oleg, it's a go . . . make it work . . . now I know why Matteo keeps you on his payroll . . . you glide untouched through the raindrops . . . thank you. . . ."

Tony and I agreed that this was our most feasible approach to extricating Max from Moscow. But we had to move quickly and pray that his partners would not learn of the plan before it was executed. Remember, once KGB, always KGB. The highest bidder prevails. Boris, Olga, and even Oleg could sell us out for more money.

"Oleg, it's a go . . . We want Max in Monaco by tomorrow night . . . no if, and, or buts . . . There will be an extra $50,000 to make it work by then . . . so get moving. . . ."

We were being quite generous with Max's money. But he would understand. All gamblers do.

We were throwing 7-11 on the first roll, no if, and, or buts!

WHERE MONEY THRIVES AND WEALTH DRIVES

Few countries share in the ostentatious ambiance as that found in Monaco. It is the most densely populated city globally, and if not the wealthiest, close to it. You name it, Monaco has it—sports, culture, opera, museums, auto racing, and gaming.

The Casino de Monte Carlo is considered one of the most exclusive in the world. Bentleys, Maseratis, Ferraris, and Mercedes are ostentatiously displayed as you approach it, signaling what's yet to confront your sensibilities when you enter the casino.

Oh, and by the way, a Porsche or two might be there for the better clients to enjoy the winding roads that encapsulate this fantastic seaside resort.

Inside the casino, most people dress chicly. It is not an environment that rewards those dressed shabbily or ill-suited for the high-octane but understated opulence that the casino looks to project.

I booked four rooms at two local hotels in Monaco. Max and Olga would stay in the same hotel as Boris and Oleg. I didn't want Max and Olga out of the sight of Boris and Oleg.

Boris complained about sharing a room with Oleg. I convinced Oleg that I wanted him to monitor Boris's behavior until Max agreed to go to London. Then Boris could get a room and enjoy Monaco and Olga on Max's dime.

Tony and I would have separate rooms in another hotel, close enough to where Max and Olga were in case of any last-minute commotions.

Whatever Boris told Olga, she had Max in Monaco the next day, just as we had instructed Oleg. They landed at Nice Cote d'Azur in France and were transported in luxury befitting Max's predilections. They were settled into their hotel rooms when Max told Olga he wanted to "try his skill" at the casino.

Olga and Max went to the Casino de Monte Carlo, followed by Boris and Oleg. Max was betting big, winning some but losing more. Money was not an object to Max. He was, as we say, "flush and satisfied."

Oleg had called us at the hotel and said he was at the casino with Olga and Max. I told him to call us when they returned to their hotel. We planned to meet Max in the lobby. Boris, Oleg, and Olga were to disappear and not return.

Olga could join Boris in his room for the remainder of their stay. Olga was never to contact Max again. She was to remove herself from his life—as if she had disappeared from the face of the earth. Or she just might!

After several hours, Olga and Max decided on dinner—their last supper. They went to some up-scale restaurant in Monaco, ate and drank like it was their last meal- at least together- and returned to the hotel. Olga peeled off as Max entered the elevator. We joined Max, to his utter dismay.

Max was puzzled. It happened so quickly that he didn't know what to think or say.

"Max, let's go to your room . . . we have a lot to talk with you about. . . ."

Max was in no shape to resist. We entered Max's room, poured ourselves a drink, and began to educate Max on what had occurred, what would happen, and why he was never returning to Moscow.

Max had a lot of trust and faith in Tony, so it was only appropriate to let Tony take the lead.

"Max, let's begin with Olga . . . Olga was KGB . . . she was not just your lover . . . but another KGB operative's lover too . . . she was part of a scheme to have you arrested for money laundering, bribery, or any other type of crime they could conjure up . . . they, being the organized crime police . . . you were headed for Siberia, Max . . . your investment in Eurokral was nothing more than a scam . . . you will never see Olga again. . . ."

Max was mortified, angry, sad, and melancholy. He started crying. Tony continued to drive the point home—"you were headed to the gulag." Tony was relentless.

I intervened at this point.

"Max, please understand . . . Tony and I had only one goal—to get you out of Moscow . . . we couldn't have cared less about your relationship with Olga until we found out that she and another KGB agent were lovers . . . isn't it better we told you and did something, than you being arrested and sitting in a jail cell somewhere in Russia? . . . We've booked you and us on the next flight out of here and back to London . . .

Max wanted to say his goodbyes to Olga. I told Max that Olga had left Monaco and was returning to Moscow.

"Max, . . . don't blame yourself, Olga, or anyone else . . . it will get you nowhere . . . nothing good would have come out of you staying in Moscow . . . you had a good run, now savor the more memorable times . . . leave while you're in love . . . it soothes the heartache. . . . never forget, feelings camouflage wise decisions . . . don't let them interfere with your judgment. . . ."

We packed Max's suitcase, loaded it into a taxi, processed through immigration and customs, and boarded the one-and-a-half-hour flight to London Heathrow.

Max is back in London, safe and sound, only to be shadowed by one of Moscow's most significant money-laundering investigations.

AN ORGANIZED KLEPTOCRACY

There is no other way to interpret the facts. By 1998, organized crime in Russia controlled fifty percent of the commercial banks, sixty percent of the public businesses, and forty percent of the private enterprises in Russia. In a communist country, these alarming statistics can only lead to one conclusion: corruption has infected the very institutions of government that should protect its people.

Estimates are only estimates because there is no way to calculate the actual amounts of money laundered through off-shore banks during the early periods of *perestroika*. It is somewhere in the 200-400 billion dollar range. Max was part of this complex yet nascent global scheme to extract wealth from the Russian economy and relocate it to the West.

After Max composed himself and pulled his thoughts and emotions together, Tony and I would visit him. My fascination with how money and wealth are transferred throughout the global behemoth of banking and stock markets led to many in-depth discussions with Max.

Max was a fountain of information once you could get him talking. His stories about living in Moscow were encyclopedic. Of course, my immediate concern was, "Max did you lose any money through your engagement with Eurokral?"

Max was more than forthcoming.

"Marty, lose money . . . don't be foolish . . . the money I made investing in Eurokral allowed me to invest in properties that I had never before contemplated . . . I learned from Ivan and my partners that there are vast differences between making money, creating wealth, and protecting your investments . . . My time in Moscow taught me more than my Oxford finance professors, who taught principles that my Russian partners discounted decades ago. . . ."

"I have real estate investments that span the globe . . . Spain, New York, Lugano, and Cornwall . . . and you will never, or should I say the government, will never find my name attached to any of these properties . . . when it comes to creating wealth, the Russians know the business better than anyone. . . ."

"But Max, were you ever threatened or scared that your life was in danger . . . that you would be arrested or tortured . . . these were some pretty rough characters . . . ?

"I know what you read in the papers paints an ugly picture . . . there may have been all of what you read occurring, but I never experienced it . . . I guess you could say my *krysha* looked after me . . . see, I even learned the Russian term for protection . . . ," Max volunteered.

"And who was that, Max . . . Daniel, Dimitri, or Ivan . . . ?"

"If I tell you, you won't believe me . . . it was a KGB agent . . . his name was Boris . . . Olga introduced me to him, and he looked after my interests . . . he taught me how to move my money around so that my partners would never know where it was . . . he was brilliant . . . He was part of the old guard that Yelstin trusted . . . many of Yelstin's advisors were bright, university-educated 'young Turks,' as they liked to be called . . . they knew the banking industry. . . . How it worked legally and could be compromised . . . as I said, Marty, I got an education and made money at the same time . . . it was less expensive than my years at Oxford. . . ."

Naturally, I was captivated by Boris being Max's *roof*. How much did Boris earn? And Olga, Marisha's cut-out in Moscow? Was Oleg in on it? Was Marisha part of the ruse? Were Tony and I taken by these fraudsters? Did Matteo have any involvement? Did he suspect anything? The questions were endless. The answers were never forthcoming.

Once again, the plot behind the plot and the recurring conspiracies are symbolic of these government and political officials, oligarchs, and their minions organizing crime.

Max would shut down and seem dejected. He missed Olga, who was never to call on Max again. Whatever Oleg did or knew, I was unlikely ever to know. Even if Oleg would share it with me, how much was believable or trustworthy?

And Marisha? Could Matteo or I ever trust her again?

Sitting with Tony and reviewing what had transpired over the last year, he reminded me never to trust the Russians.

"What did I tell you from the beginning Marty . . . there is always a plot behind the plot . . . behind the plot . . . I never trusted Marisha . . . Oleg was out of a movie script . . . Max was caught up in a mid-life crisis that he didn't understand . . . and we have an invoice to collect . . . over to half a million euros. . . ."

"Tony, I'll leave that up to you . . . you know Max better than I do . . . will he balk if we present him with an invoice and do not itemize the costs? . . . the $250,000 to Oleg may upset him . . . he may question it, and I'm not sure we should drag him through the weeds . . . simply refer to it as an extraction cost . . . the remaining costs are insignificant and can be documented if he demands to see them. . . ."

Tony was non-pulsed over presenting Max with the invoice. He would cushion the blow because Max would have been the fall guy had this money-laundering scheme been prosecuted. Moreover, Max made a killing, not literally, of course, in his investment. He was unlikely to play Scrooge with Tony—and he didn't.

He had the monies transferred into Tony's account from a bank in Jersey. Tony, nor did I ask any questions. We, too, were educated in the ways and means of the Russian oligarchs and how they make and maintain their wealth instead of earning a living.

"We pretend to work, you pretend to pay us" had a new meaning for me, but I suspect for Tony as well.

Over the next two decades, the extent of wealth extraction from Russia, the imprisonment of oligarchs who refused to play ball with Putin, and the assassinations and attempted killings of Putin's enemies on sovereign territories became more relevant to Max, Tony, and me.

Putin executed a strategy that propelled him onto the world stage. He was a player in geopolitics, intent on bringing back respect and dignity to the former empire once known as the Soviet Union. Or, as President Ronald Reagan called it, an Evil Empire.

Tony and I have visited Max over the years. He nostalgically reflects on this unanticipated interlude in his life. He never talks about Olga. And he continues to smoke those awful, cheap cigars. I suspect he doesn't want to see his wealth go up in smoke.

In 2019, I visited Tony before he passed away. On my return to the States, I diverted to Port Issac to visit my Australian friends on holiday.

As I regaled the locals at the Port Gaverne Hotel about the dirty Russian money polluting London, one asked me if I knew the Russian oligarch who owned this sprawling mansion sitting on the cliff, steps from the hotel.

I thought of Maximillian Powis, his investments, and his mention of Cornwall.

Max's spirit and his legacy live. That mansion will always bring back memories of this incredible journey into another abyss.

THE SHARKS SMELL MONEY—
LOTS OF IT

A prospective client approached me just when I thought I was over dealing with Russian shysters. He was involved in an industry that I knew very little about—the taxi industry. I suspect that most people have no idea how this industry works and, more importantly, how this industry is structured to encourage investment by money launderers.

I never realized what a cash cow it was for the unscrupulous operators who took advantage of the drivers, cozied up to the regulators, and played ball with the politicians who lived off their campaign contributions. It was the perfect *vehicle* for Russian gangsters to launder their money.

There are few environments as competitive as that of New York City. Asked by a "friend of a friend" to conduct due diligence on a fledging taxi and limousine company, I thought nothing of it. Although the taxi company's owner was a Russian, Alexander Lithkov, little did I think this was another scheme to capture the lion's share of the taxi industry by persons involved with a top Russian gangster.

Roman Illif was considered a boss of Russian organized crime in New York. Illif immigrated to New York in the 1970s and settled in Brighton Beach. His specialty was extortion, torture, and murder. He had been arrested several times but never convicted. Witnesses either refused to testify, disappeared, were brutally assaulted, or were killed. His reputation in the Russian émigré community was legendary and vicious.

A violent reputation was the gold standard for a Russian mobster. It's often referred to as the "value of a bad reputation." Most Russians learn that the police are not their friend at a young age. The police are nothing more than muscle for the local crime bosses or out-and-out extortionists. There was little cooperation between the police and the community.

Illif was not only involved in strong-arming; he was considered a master at taking over legitimate businesses so that he could launder money on behalf of Russians both here and abroad.

To those in the Russian émigré community, taxation was another way for the government to get their greedy hands into the pockets of those who toiled relentlessly to make a living. Any business that overwhelmingly relied on cash was a worthwhile investment. The taxi industry is an industry ripe for criminal exploitation.

The key or weak spot in the industry is the financing mechanism. The government's outdated regulatory system makes the taxi industry especially vulnerable. Artificially constraining the number of medallions (i.e., licenses) increases the medallion value. The only value of that little piece of metal affixed to the hood of those yellow taxis is what the government decides it is worth. It is a system established in the 1930s and has seen little reform until Uber and Lyft entered the market.

Prospective investors could easily purchase the medallions from the city through a corporation or limited liability company, usually registered in Delaware. Initially, investors demonstrated financial solvency to the government regulators, who were less than enthusiastic or skilled in determining the sources of the monies. In the interest of regulatory efficiency, the City ultimately removed this requirement. It was merely concerned with receiving their cut in taxes, administrative costs, and likely any other unreportable (i.e., under-the-table) fees.

Once invested in the industry, the investor solicits legitimate financial institutions for loans, using the medallions as collateral. The investor has a means of comingling dirty money with clean money, essentially avoiding all the "red flags" that identify a money launderer.

It is the ideal regulatory scheme to promote institutionalized corruption. Selling medallions became a robust revenue stream for the City.

My client, a lending institution, was solicited by Lithkov to underwrite the costs of medallions. The purchase of a medallion was in the neighborhood of $200,000. Lithkov had qualified for a ten million-dollar loan, using as collateral 50 medallions he owned. The client was suspicious and heard rumors that Litkov was involved with Russian gangsters in New York and Moscow.

My client's concern was that he might violate the money laundering statutes—an investigative mantra that had taken on a life of its own by this time. Performing reasonable due diligence was one requirement of the money laundering protocols applied to financial institutions.

Naturally, the first person I contacted was Michael Savage. Savage, as you might remember, was the former New York City cop who was the expert on the Russian mafia in New York.

When I mentioned Lithkov's name to Savage, he responded, "Marty; he's a player . . . his godfather is Roman Illif, the boss of the Chechen mafia in Brighton Beach . . . what is it with you? . . . do you have any clients who aren't Russian?

"Michael, in this instance, my client is a lending institution . . . I'm on the side of the angels this time. . . ." At least, that's what I thought.

When it came to Brighton Beach and the Russian mafia, few were more knowledgeable than Savage. My other resource was a retired Customs agent, James Davis, who had devoted the last ten years of his career investigating the Russian mafia.

I also reached out to Palmisano and McComb. Knowing McComb's interest in the Russian émigré community, I now felt that he would co-operate with me if I could provide him with information on Lithkov or Illif. As we would say in the business, "one hand washes the other."

"Jack, this is Marty . . . remember me?"

"Of course, Marty . . . how's it going?"

"Jack, I have a client . . . it's a financial institution involving a Russian who travels back and forth to Moscow . . . I thought it might interest you. . . . ?

"What's his name?"

"Alexander Lithkov."

There were several moments of silence. Jack suggested that we meet at a discreet location. He no longer wanted to speak over the phone. I'm unsure whether Jack was overly cautious and dramatic or the CIA monitored the phones.

I suggest we meet in a small café in SoHo. Jack agreed to meet later in the afternoon or early evening. I was comfortable with that.

The fact that Jack entertained a meeting implied that he was interested in Lithkov. He knew the name. That he chose to meet the same day indicated his interest in Lithkov was more than fleeting. The trick now was to get more information than I could give. Jack, I am sure, had a similar motive.

"Marty, good to see you again . . . you still speaking with Marisha?"

"Of course, Jack . . . you should know . . . I'm sure you're still monitoring her calls. . . ."

There was no doubt that McComb was looking for information on Marisha. There was nothing I could tell him that he didn't know. But at least I had something to trade. How valuable it was, my instincts would have to tell.

Jack snickered when I responded as if he knew I knew.

"Marisha is in Prague, living with Matteo . . . she is part of Matteo's business . . . you may even know one of Matteo's assets, Oleg?"

I remembered that McComb gave me a phone number of an embassy employee, who I figured was CIA. McComb would know Oleg. There was little doubt in my mind.

"Of course, we know Oleg . . . he's KGB . . . , Marty."

"But let's talk about Lithkov . . . that's what we're both here for . . . not to rehash what we know, Marty."

"Jack, let's make this short and sweet . . . I know very little about him . . . he is of interest to my client, who is in the financial industry . . . my client does not want to get caught up in a money-laundering scam and have his company sanctioned . . . I'd appreciate any help you could give me. . . ."

"Okay, I will share this with you, but you must promise me that you will not tell anyone where you got it . . . it could trigger an internal that I don't need. . . ."

I thought, is Jack for real? Does he genuinely believe that I believe what he gave me had not been cleared by his superiors, and he was tacitly recruiting me as an asset? This was classic CIA. Make me think I am special.

"No problem Jack . . . your fingerprints will be nowhere near this. . . ."

"Lithkov was born on the outskirts of Moscow. . . . a town called Kuntsevo . . . He emigrated to the United States when he was ten years old. . . . He lived in Brighton Beach with his father and mother. . . .

Although his parents encouraged him to go to college and become a lawyer, Lithkov had a silver tongue and was destined to cut his path as a gifted grifter. . . . He was always looking to make a fast buck . . . He had traveled to Moscow one summer and, while there, met with several members of the Duma—Russia's Congress. He was introduced to them by the local priest, who had relatives in Brighton Beach. . . ."

Only later did I find out that this local priest in Moscow also knew Father Portonosky.

After listening to Jack's litany of information on Lithkov, there was no doubt that he had an open investigation. There was also no doubt that McComb was sharing this information at the behest of higher-ups. Lithkov was a target of the CIA.

I then raised the name Roman Illif. There was a deafening silence. Even a CIA agent with all his training could not camouflage his body language. I struck a chord.

"Marty, you don't want to go there . . . he is one mean mother-fucker . . . we know about him, but I can't share anything with you . . . just be careful . . . *these* are bad actors . . . they kill. . . ."

McComb punctuated his response in the plural, leading me to believe that Illif was part of a more extensive criminal network that had its roots in Moscow. McComb was not willing to go there with me. We left the meeting under amicable terms, with McComb saying, "Marty, I expect to hear from you . . . you gave me nothing . . . I unloaded . . . "

I had to contact Marisha for no reason but to assuage my curiosity. I knew where this was leading—-and it wasn't good.

I met with the client and essentially told him what I had uncovered. He was unpulsed.

"Marty, understand something, we make money from lending . . . that is our bread and butter. . . . We are not in the business of chasing gangsters . . . unless you can show me how Lithkov gets his money or explain that he is mixed up in the rackets, we are not paying you to play Elliott Ness. . . ."

"No problem . . . let us work on this a little longer . . . I will get back to you when I think we have something in your best interests to discuss."

In this business, you learn that the client's always right even when they're wrong. "Willful blindness" has sanctions, sometimes quite severe.

I realized I had to enlist Dasha's services, possibly Marisha and Matteo. I had to build an irrefutable dossier on Lithkov and Illif that would cause the client to pause.

As we began sniffing around, we started to get pushback from the Taxi and Limousine Commission, which made little sense. Why would they be concerned about Lithkov all of a sudden? For years, they showed no interest in how he was buying medallions through his shell company. Now that he is searching for legitimate financing, they are getting excited. Makes no sense?

It became increasingly apparent that the Commission was a patronage pit staffed by political appointees who knew little about the financial aspects or nuances of the industry. I was certainly far from being an expert on the industry; however, it was evident that the source of financing was a regulatory juggernaut in my short time making inquiries. It was rife with money laundering on a massive scale and all sorts of fraud.

The longer I've been in this business, the more I learn what I don't know. If there's a gimmick to swindle money out of the unsuspecting, there's always a group of grifters who have it figured out.

But to have the government enable grifters is another question. Precisely that's what happened. It's why we were getting blowback from the Commission, a fact we only found out years later.

Taxi drivers were extended loans from greedy banks and financial institutions. Immigrants who barely understood English, never mind reading loan documents and the fine print, were given loans to purchase medallions with little or no money.

The value of the medallions' was artificially inflated through a practice known as "manipulative wash trading." The lending institutions were refinancing the loans, attaching outrageous administrative fees. It was a Ponzi scheme in which the banks, government, taxi owners, and brokers were complicit.

Of course, at the time, I had no idea that my client might eventually be implicated in these predatory lending practices. So much for being on the side of the angels.

WELCOME TO THE VOLCANO

Back to Brighton Beach, Dasha and I go. Every trip to Brighton Beach was a learning experience. You can never learn too much. Spending time in the bowels of the Russian underworld is an experience no amount of formal education can compete with.

Lithkov lived in a rustic village in upstate New York—Katonah. Among its residents were actors, television personalities, and real estate moguls. Lithkov insinuated himself into the community, hoping the shine would rub off. Lithkov was engaged in what is known as reputation laundering. Fortunately, he was far too coarse, culturally challenged, and unsophisticated to be accepted into this rarified community. It was all about the image of affluence, not the cultural baggage that comes with lineage and breeding. His money allowed him to hob-knob with the well-to-do's. Of course, he mistook money for wealth, never understanding that wealth whispers, money squeals.

It was time to access the gray market. I contacted my guy in Florida to obtain Lithkov's telephone tolls from his home in Katonah, his apartment, and his office in New York City. Few records are more telling than who you speak with daily. They define your social and professional networks.

Developing sources who knew Lithkov was Dasha's *forte*. She knew people in the Russian community and could sniff around without signaling our interest to Kishlov. It was just a matter of time before she developed something.

I stayed in touch with Savage and Davis, salvaging whatever information may have come across on Lithkov. Additionally, I had several sources in the FBI and the New York City Police Department knowledgeable in Russian organized crime.

I also reached out to Marisha. She never wavered when it came to helping me in an investigation. She anticipated a plane ticket across the big pond to New York. Lithkov's escapades in Moscow could prove interesting, especially to my skeptical client.

"Marisha, I dreaded making this call, but I had to . . . I need to speak to you . . . preferably in a secure location. . . ."

"You mean I'm coming to New York?"

"I thought it was time to pay back Matteo for all he did for me in Prague . . . would you and Matteo like to come to the Volcano . . . ?"

"What's the Volcano, Marty . . . Mount Edna in Sicily?"

"Close Marisha . . . only it's New York City . . . and it could blow any minute . . . it's a phrase that we in the business use when describing New York . . . comes out of a book you may have never read . . . Boss of Bosses . . . you can put this in your repertoire. . . ."

"When would you like me to book the flight?"

"Marisha, let me make it clear . . . the flights . . . for you and Matteo . . . have Matteo call me so we can arrange a mutually-agreeable time . . . but soon, very soon. . . ."

"I will . . . can't wait to see New York . . . It's always been my dream . . . and knowing you will show me around makes it even special. . . ."

"And Matteo, too, Marisha."

I knew this would be complicated. What wouldn't I do for the unassailable mistress? Intrigue, curiosity, danger, and money drove me. And perhaps, not in that order?

The following day, Matteo called. I explained the situation and how I could use Marisha in the Brighton Beach area. As a bonafide Russian well-connected to the communist *nomenklatura*, she would be the perfect beard for Dasha. Of course, Dasha was part of my problem.

How Marisha and Dasha would get along posed an issue. Marisha seemed to have a problem with other women. I never understood her resentment toward Guisipinna, but I was never there to witness the personal dynamics.

When she arrived, I had to make it clear to Marisha that we were a team. We must work together. She can not allow personal issues to distract us from our delicate work. My client had deep pockets, and so long as we delivered a credible product, the client would pay.

"Matteo, when can you and Marisha get here . . . the sooner, the better . . . ?"

"Can you give me two weeks . . . I need to clear the calendar. . . ."

"No problem Matteo . . . but I can't fly you both first or business class . . . it has to be coach, but upgrade if you wish . . . Marisha can make up the difference in her billables. . . ."

"Great, Marty . . . looking forward to our trip to the Volcano. . . ."

I could see that Marisha had already educated Matteo on our conversation. Now he was referring to New York City as The Volcano.

A week went by, and my guy from Florida called me. He had three months of telephone calls from Lithkov's residences and office. The hard part was analyzing the phone calls to determine those that may yield valuable information.

I contacted a former intelligence analyst I worked with previously and asked if she would mind doing some work for me. I needed an analysis of phone calls, particularly those that may have piqued the interests of a savvy intelligence analyst. She agreed, and I sent her Lithkov's calls.

With Marisha and Matteo arriving at JFK International in another week, I arranged their lodging and excursions. It had to be done in such a way as to camouflage their contact with me. I was concerned that McComb, Lithkov, or Illif might be surveilling her. And, of course, there was Dasha.

Before Matteo and Marisha departed, I told Marisha to do her homework on Roman Illif. I wanted to know as much about him and his network as possible—but do it discreetly. *"No fingerprints, Marisha."*

"That's always understood with you, Marty . . . you never want to have your fingerprints on anything, including me. . . ."

I ignored her remarks and merely stated, "Nobody knows that better than you, Marisha . . . you were taught that at a young age in Moscow . . . touch*é*. . . ."

Arranging for lodging in Brighton Beach could be problematic. Everybody knew everybody, and I was sure Marisha would be the topic of scuttlebutt and rumors. Teaming her up with Dasha, who could be Marisha's cousin, might remove some suspicions. Who knew? It was a long shot.

I had Dasha make the lodging arrangements in Brighton Beach. I would find a safe house in Manhattan where she and Matteo could rendezvous. It could serve as our base of operations as well.

With the arrival of Matteo and Marisha in a few short days, I sat down with Dasha and discussed the game plan. She understood my previous relationship with Marisha and had no problem with it. She had a new Russian beau and was content with her newfound love. I told Dasha that she had to deal with Marisha delicately—that Marisha was "hard work."

"Remember, Marisha is an only child . . . she was the apple of her father's eye . . . the world revolves around her . . . her wants and needs . . . Dasha, the term 'entitled' describes Marisha the best. . . ."

Dasha understood what to expect.

"Marty, do I get hazardous duty pay for this . . . I'm not sure who is more dangerous . . . Illif, Lithkov, or Marisha?"

We both laughed simultaneously.

Realizing that McComb may know that Marisha and Matteo were traveling to the United States, I contacted him to tell him what he already knew.

"Nothing surprising there . . . thank's for the heads-up . . . you are so accommodating, Marty."

I didn't know whether he was being sarcastic or serious. But neither did it matter. His trailing Marisha would likely enhance her cachet in the Russian émigré community, providing it was detected.

Driving to JFK International with Dasha allowed me to educate her about Marisha's pedigree. They needed to trust one another, as their safety depended on a shared sense of their respective histories. Marisha's lifetime affiliation with the Communist Party was relevant. "Once KGB, always KGB," I impressed this on Dasha. She understood. Her background was in Ukraine. She knew all about the KGB.

Their flight from Prague was two hours late. By the time they cleared Customs and Immigration, Dasha and I had consumed too much alcohol to drive to Manhattan. I booked three rooms at the Marriott Hotel, left the car in the short-term parking lot, and we taxied to the hotel with Matteo and Marisha.

They were exhausted. Upon seeing me, Marisha hugged me and said, "Marty, you made my dream come true . . . you brought me to New York. . . ."

It was clear that this was for Matteo's and Dasha's benefit. Leave it to Marisha to throw hand grenades!

We checked in, and Matteo and Marisha ordered room service. Dasha and I had dinner in the dining room and retired to our separate rooms for the night.

We met in the lobby the following day, had breakfast, taxied to the car, and drove to Manhattan. I booked their rooms at a boutique hotel in the Village—The Washington Square Hotel. It was several blocks from Sal Persico's office. I wanted Sal to meet Marisha and Matteo—especially Matteo, who did most of the work on Turgay Gallick's investigation. Moreover, we could use his office for meetings, which, if trailed, would serve as a convenient excuse for Marisha and Dasha. Sal's representation of the Mafia would be easily discovered by those curious.

After checking Marisha and Matteo into the hotel, a Village tour was on the agenda. I knew Marisha would enjoy Caffee Reggio. The storied history of this coffee house was one of the left-wing and Marxist students, activists, and professors gathering together to champion the cause of communism.

Then there was the White Horse Tavern, where the literary giants of the 1800 and 1900s opined about the state of affairs, traded labor union stories, and mixed and mingled with the waterfront thugs that frequented the bar to "wet their whistle."

And we finished up at the infamous Umberto's Clam House in Little Italy, where the mobster Joseph Gallo was gunned down on the sidewalk. There Marisha would dine on calamari, the Italian version of caviar. We laughed, of course.

It would not be complete without a cannoli and expresso at LaBella Ferrara, across from Il Cortile, where the Mafia held initiation ceremonies in the basement.

It was too much information for Marisha or Matteo to digest in one day. Their heads were bursting. I was enjoying the day's electricity as much as they were. You can never get bored in the Volcano. It is a city filled with more anecdotes than the world is with people.

With all its character and intimacy, Prague was a small town compared to New York City. In Prague, Marisha and Matteo were big fish in a small pond. In New York City, they were small fish in a big pond.

And Brighton Beach would be another story.

NEVER UNDERESTIMATE THE VALUE
OF THE USEFUL IDIOT(S)

I made it clear to Marisha that she had to enlist her KGB talents.

"Always assume you are being tailed, the phone in the hotel or wherever is tapped, there are 'bugs" in the hotel room or at the table where you are eating, and you will be tested on how well you lie."

In other words, let paranoia set in. Brighton Beach is not a democracy. It is a replica of an authoritarian state, only much smaller and compact.

I educated her on the players in Brighton Beach. Father Portonosky would be a good source of information. She knew the shills in Moscow who were laundering monies on behalf of the Communist Party and the church. I informed her about Portonosky's bingo operation and how the church used it to launder money. Marisha understood all too well.

Off to Brighton Beach, Marisha and Dasha would go. I knew that Marisha could deliver if she didn't allow her emotional liabilities to take over. She was well-educated and schooled in the craft of deceit and trickery.

Before long, Marisha and Dasha met the mobsters that populated the nightclubs, strip joints, and after-hours clubs. Both Marisha's and Dasha's looks attracted one particular strip club operator.

According to Savage, the club is owned by Illif but not on paper. It would not be long before Marisha, and Dasha would expect to perform sexually. Marisha, non-pulsed, plainly informed the strip club owner that her partner, Matteo, was connected to the Italian Mafia.

Dasha was matter-of-fact—fuck off!

Marisha was not shy about mentioning the name of Sal Persico, who she positioned as Matteo's attorney. Ironically, the relationship between

Sal and Anthony Pellegrino and his representation of mobsters involved in the fuel tax scams would play well among the Russian gangsters.

Sal would have been furious had he known that Marisha played the Mafia card. Sal had no desire to be implicated in this undercover operation. But Marisha was a survivor. She played whatever role worked at the moment. Classic KGB.

Before too long, Marisha and Dasha had established a rapport with the strip club owner, who was not the "sharpest knife in the draw." Marisha liked that idiom too. He was shooting his mouth off, telling Marisha about all the money made on healthcare and stock frauds, the women he was running through his club as dancers, and the cash he was laundering through his club. He tried to impress Marisha and Dasha, but he did the opposite. They could see what a fool he was. Marisha had his measure and played him—a refined trait that always lingered in the back of my mind.

When Marisha probed into what he knew about the taxi-cab scams, foolishly, he opened up like the gates of the Hoover Dam. And wouldn't you know it, he knew Lithkov, who would spend afternoons in his club, throwing his money around. Lithkov's weakness was, among other things, women.

Lithkov would go to "the Beach" to avoid Manhattan, where he had an apartment with his wife. He portrayed himself as happily married and a family man, but his hyde came out when he was away from his backyard. He was a wealthy, coarse, unsophisticated reprobate. A so-called *nouveau riche* oligarch. Money could not disguise his unsavory character. Class is one thing money can't buy.

As I knew, Marisha would deliver. And Dasha was there to confirm everything Marisha had learned. We would have irrefutable evidence if Marisha could acquire physical proof, like a conversation with either the strip club owner or Lithkov. It would also preclude any defense of "plausible deniability," not exactly in the client's best interest.

How far to push the envelope was a decision that we felt Sal should be *informally* involved in? There were many legal implications as well as practical issues. We didn't wish to "burn" Marisha and Dasha. Their physical well-being and long-term value were strategically-important.

And Sal was representing clients involved in the fuel-tax scam. It was complex. Then again, if it was easy, the client didn't need us.

I arranged a meeting with Sal at his office. Sal was always accommodating, realizing a new client may be in the offing. And the Russians had money to throw around. There was no downside.

Sal's charisma was infectious. Everyone that met him marveled at how he presented himself. Confident but not arrogant. A pronounced New York accent, but not thuggish. His dress was meticulous. It made him effective before a jury or arranging a plea bargain with hungry prosecutors. He knew how to lower the temperature.

We sat around his long mahogany table in his book-lined conference room. For whatever reason, mahogany seemed to be the decades' color, making everything look rich and intimate. Sal opened up the meeting, charming Matteo and Marisha.

"Matteo, I must thank you for all your help in the matter Marty brought to you . . . had it not been for your connections in Prague, we may not have been as successful . . . you were the lynchpin in that investigation . . . hopefully Marty compensated you appropriately?"

"I was only happy to help Marty and you . . . it made me money as well . . . and of course, it got me to New York, and I met the love of my life, Marisha . . . it was all good, Sal."

"And you, Marisha . . . I have heard so many good things about you . . . I'm happy that you are enjoying this line of work . . . not only is it lucrative, but you are helping those the government would thrash if it weren't for the rule of law. . . ."

I knew before Sal could say anymore, Marisha interrupted.

"Can I call you Sal or Mr. Persico?"

"Sal is certainly appropriate in our situation. . . ."

"Your point is well-taken, Sal, but I was under the impression that your government is of, by, and for the people . . . why would it thrash the rights of the people . . . ?"

I decided this would end up in a philosophical debate, so I "cut to the chase." Another idiom for Marisha.

"We are here to discuss our legal options . . . should we capture conversations on tape or memorialize the conversation in writing? . . ."

Sal's reluctance to opine on this was noticeable. He finally said, " be careful what you wish for . . . taping can be a double-edged sword . . . it will also expose Marisha and Dasha, which I think you may not want to do?"

"And your client would be in an untenable position . . . he could no longer claim plausible deniability . . . the government would argue willful blindness. . . ."

It was evident that Sal saw the legal implications if this due diligence found its way into a courtroom. The tapes and even the notes would be discoverable and expose Marisha and Dasha to cross-examination and possibly retaliation.

We all agreed that there would be no electronic taping, only notes we'd sanitize into a report for the client. All notes would then be discarded.

As the meeting concluded, Sal suggested we go to Babbo, the latest Italian restaurant to open in the Village. It received rave reviews from the "foodies" and maestros of the New York culinary scene.

Matteo and Marisha weren't shy about the wines they chose. Barolo's and Spanish Rijioas were high on their list. Sal was partial to Italian wines, Barolos, and Amarones. Dasha and I took a more measured approach, surveying the evolving dynamics.

Listening to every word spoken and watching the body language tell much about what others think. Sal was intrigued by Marisha. Matteo was under Marisha's spell. And Dasha sent out trial balloons to see how the others would react.

Dinner went well. Of course, I picked up the tab and thanked Sal for his legal insights. Sal taxied home. Marisha and Matteo disappeared into the night. Dasha met up with her partner. And I retired to my apartment, contemplating our next move.

As I reflected on what we knew and where the due diligence would require additional information, I realized that Marisha had not provided any information on Roman Illif. Illif had connections in Moscow as well as in Brighton Beach. Did Marisha merely forget, being excited about her trip to New York? Or did she purposely ignore following up on Illif? I addressed it the following day.

"Marisha, where are you on Illif and his connections in Moscow?"

I could feel that Marisha was a bit uncomfortable answering me.

"Marty, I knew you would ask me at some point . . . I wasn't avoiding it . . . I was trying to figure out how I would answer you. . . ."

"Truthfully, I would hope, Marisha?"

"Illif is the Party's representative for bringing money to America . . . he is their guy in New York he was a rising star in the Party . . . he was Party's man in the Chechnya . . . his name is legendary . . . I know because my family knew him personally . . . when it came to moving money throughout Europe, he was their man . . . he is skilled, trusted, and ruthless. . . ."

"Marisha, when were you gonna tell me this? . . . why did you wait till I asked you?"

"I felt that it would hurt my relationship with you and Matteo . . . I didn't want you to think poorly of me . . . Illif and his group were my parent's friends . . . the Party was like a God to them . . . I must admit that I was conflicted . . . I was hoping the issue would disappear . . . it didn't . . .

I suspected Illif had laundered money on behalf of Marisha's family, which of course, made her conflicted in several ways.

I realized that Marisha, no different from anyone else, had deeply-held loyalties and beliefs that she could not discard or share for fear of being ostracized and rejected by her newfound colleagues. We have all been there. As I said to Marisha, "There but for the Grace of God go I." Another idiom for her dictionary. No further discussion was necessary.

It was apparent that her role in Brighton Beach was no longer tenable. We would discontinue this phase of our inquiry.

I received a call from the intelligence analyst reviewing Illif and Lithkov's telephone calls. She had identified about twenty calls that she felt deserved follow-up.

I contacted my source in Florida and asked him to see if he could obtain the subscribers. There were many calls to Moscow that Matteo or Marisha could follow up on.

Marisha got right on it. She called her contacts in Moscow. As she had anticipated, the calls were to higher-ups in the Communist Party. There was no doubt that McComb and the CIA were well aware of these calls and the subsequent conversations. Equally, I was sure the conversations were carefully sanitized. Nonetheless, the calls were additional fodder for us to include in our due diligence. Indeed, the CIA knew of Lithkov and Illif's "investments."

"WE'RE IN THE BUSINESS OF MAKING MONEY, NOT CHASING OLIGARCHS"

—The Client

It was time to regroup and determine what we knew, what we didn't know, what information we needed, and how to address it with the client. By this time, we knew that the client would only entertain a factual finding that Lithkov was laundering money on behalf of Russian gangsters. We knew Lithkov was nestled in the Brighton Beach underworld and had a relationship with Illif. Whether or not that was sufficient for the client to refuse to lend money to Lithkov was a moral judgment and a financial decision.

How much public humiliation was the client willing to accept before he would reject Lithkov's application for millions of dollars? Moreover, what were the probabilities that Lithkov would renege on the loans, file for personal bankruptcy, or reorganize the corporate entity? I contacted the client to arrange a meeting.

We agreed to meet in Sal's office. I would bring Marisha to the meeting for no reason other than to reinforce the lengths we had gone to ascertain the extent of Lithkov's involvement in the Russian underworld. Her accent and connections to the Kremlin hierarchy would illuminate and provide the dramatic optics that might influence the client's decision.

I walked a fine line between an investigator providing the bare facts and an advocate for or against the client's ultimate decision. Nonetheless, I was hedging my bet against any blowback from the client if anything went sour.

Meeting in Sal's office was also a strategic decision. Including Sal in the meeting might result in the client retaining Sal to avoid future litigation or mitigate any blowback down the road. Moreover, Sal had "no skin in the game," another idiom for Marisha. His candid opinion would hold sway with the client.

I contacted the client. We met in Sal's office the following week. That meant that Marisha and Matteo could savor all the City offered. And they did. Broadway shows, museums, and indulging in the lounges and nightclubs gave them a flavor of why New York City retains its status as the epicenter of the Western world. They were mesmerized. New York had all the charm, excitement, and grit they had always read about and were finally experiencing.

We did the typical touristy things, such as the Empire State Building, the Statue of Liberty, and the neighborhoods, such as Harlem, Hell's Kitchen, Wall Street, Little Italy, and Ground Zero, under reconstruction. They were especially interested in seeing where the infamous John Gotti hung out, so I took them past the Ravenite Social Club. They witnessed Gotti's thugs guarding the club and watching for the feds.

Marisha was a fine and rare arts aficionado. I arranged for her to take a private tour of the JP Morgan Library and Museum, which housed the three Gutenberg Bibles, the only library with this exclusive collection.

We had a whirlwind week that accomplished as much as possible in this relatively narrow window. What lay ahead was always on my mind. We were only a day away from meeting with the client. I had to present a convincing argument to give the client what he had requested but not advocate a position.

The night before the scheduled meeting, I called Sal. We discussed the approach. I would introduce Sal as our corporate legal counsel. That provided my firm lawyer-client privilege if there was any blowback from either the client or Lithkov.

I realized that this meeting with the client was make-or-break. Our fees had nearly tripled from what we initially believed this due diligence would cost. The costs associated with the travel of Marisha and Matteo to the states, housing them, arranging for lodging for Dasha and Marisha in Brighton Beach, and the ancillary expenses blew the initial budget.

Regardless, we had no other options. The client demanded thorough due diligence. Anything less than expected would be grounds to reject our findings, with financially catastrophic consequences. It was why I was reluctant to take these Russian engagements. They never seemed to result in a black-or-white resolution. The final result was always murky. Then again, "If it were easy, they (i.e., the client) don't need us."

Sal agreed to sit and listen, providing no legal advice to the client. He was not the client's counsel. Nor was he an advocate in one way or another. He was merely there to address any concerns I may have had, or the client was interested in regarding the due diligence.

Starting the meeting at 11 A.M. strategically allowed us to break at 12:30 for lunch. This would allow us time to regroup if the temperature rises and the client is uncooperative or demanding. Sal was always thinking of plan B or an exit strategy.

Marisha was, of course, getting a lesson in strategic posturing. Decisions made before the meeting can be more critical than during the session. They will shape the outcome. Another tutorial and tuition-free; the client and I bore the costs.

Arriving at precisely 11 A.M., I greeted the client. I introduced Sal to the client. The client's response still resonates in my head.

"I know who you are, Mr. Persico. Your reputation precedes you . . . several of <u>our</u> friends are quite enamored with your legal talents . . . that Marty has you as his corporate attorney speaks well for his judgment. . . ."

"You need not call me Mr. Persico; Sal will do . . . and thank you for that unsolicited compliment . . . Marty is my client and a friend for the past 30 years. . . ."

I knew at this point that Sal had ingratiated himself with the client. The fact that they had mutual "friends" was an unexpected bonus. But the client immediately went on offense.

"Marty, I want to make something clear . . . my firm is in the business of making money through lending money . . . we are not in the business of chasing oligarchs . . . we are not here to listen to Russian mafia stories that seem to always end with Jewish surnames . . . we have two criteria: is the client solvent and can the client provide the collateral necessary to protect our investment? If the answer to those two questions is yes, we need to go no further. . . ."

I could see that this would be a contentious meeting. The client was determined to make the loan to Lithkov regardless of what I said.

However, there was one thing the client conveniently ignored. Knowing your customer or KYC in the industry is central to any defense if a financial firm engages in a money-laundering scheme. This standard requirement will cause a financial institution severe sanctions if ignored.

"I would suggest that the law is not as cavalier or as generous as you suggest," I politely responded.

"If I may, and I don't mean to tell you how to run your business, but the Financial Industry Regulatory Authority (FINRA) was established to quote 'safeguard the investing public against fraud and bad practices. . . . Rule 2090 is pretty clear . . . Every member shall use reasonable due diligence, in regard to opening and maintenance of every account, to know (and retain) the essential facts concerning every customer and concerning the authority of each person acting on behalf of such customer.'"

Sal remained pensive through this interchange. I realized I had intruded upon Sal's turf when I started quoting the law. But Sal was not there to represent my client's interests. He was there to represent my interests.

In the presence of my attorney, I had now put the client on notice that he had more to consider than solvency and collateral. "Reasonable due diligence" and the "essential facts" were the overriding words, not evidence beyond a reasonable doubt or any doubt. I would give him the "essential facts."

"If I may, I'd like to introduce my colleague Marisha who I seconded from Moscow and Prague . . . she works for my subsidiary in Prague . . . her specialty is Russian financial due diligence . . . her bonafide reaches deep into the Kremlin, having spent her childhood and early adult years there . . . without going too deep into her background, suffice it to say, she is what you might say "a friend of friends" . . . she knows the landscape better than anyone . . . Marisha, if I say anything incorrect or not consistent with what we learned, feel free to interject and correct me. . . ."

Marisha nodded yes and introduced herself to the client. Her Russian accent solidified her bonafide and added to her cachet. Now Lithkov's persona was stripped bare.

"Let me begin by giving you a bit of his background. Alexander Lithkov is a Russian émigré from a small village outside of Moscow. He was ten years old when his mother, father, two brothers, and sister took residence in Brighton Beach. Alexander was unlike his brothers insofar as he saw academics as the slow road to success . . . he was much more adventuresome and risk-taking . . . he mingled with the tough kids of Brighton Beach and relished the gangsters that had beautiful women, nice cars, access to the nightclubs, and always seemed to have money. He was not a tough guy . . . he was more cerebral when looking for financial gimmicks and opportunities . . . but he knew and grew up with the players of Brighton Beach . . . he dreamed of making it big one day . . . I'll let Marisha take it from here. . . ."

My client was impatient and interrupted. "There is nothing you told me that would make Alexander Lithkov a risk . . . he sounds like the classic American success story . . . was he ever arrested or convicted of a crime?

"No, he was never arrested . . . he has no criminal convictions . . . but that in and of itself does not satisfy the KYC requirements . . . for example, where did he get his money to buy 50 medallions that he is now using as cascading collateral for a ten million dollar loan?"

"You tell me," the client retorted. "That's what I'm paying you for."

It was apparent that the temperature was rising. Sal's lunch break was looking better and better. The client was unimpressed so far. Then again, the meat of the presentation was yet to come. Perhaps lunch, a Cuban, and cognac would relax the atmosphere.

Sal conveniently and timely suggested that we order lunch. Sal's secretary placed the order, and while waiting, Sal initiated a conversation with my client. The client raised several names, all Mafia, that he knew Sal would know. Sal responded in kind, never breaching his lawyer-client relationship. Had I not known better, Sal solicited the client subtly and cleverly.

As lunch arrived, I saw that the client and Sal had a rapport. Give Sal another thirty minutes, and Sal would have him "eating out of his hands." Another idiom for Marisha.

We were all relaxed, finishing lunch, when Sal went to his humidor and took out three Cubans. "Marisha, I'd offer you one, but Marty said you didn't smoke."

Marisha just smiled and said she didn't. "I'll tolerate the boys having their time together; male bonding, isn't that what you call it . . . ? . . . But I will have a cognac if I may?"

Sal, the client, and I went outside and enjoyed the Cuban while Marisha and Sal's secretary kibitzed. When we returned to complete our presentation, Sal had coopted the client. He had lowered the temperature—classic Sal.

Marisha was now prepared to deliver her part in a refined Russian accent. The optics were kicking in.

"There are two areas of concern that I uncovered during my due diligence . . . I was tasked with determining Alexander Lithkov's relationships with the Moscow and Brighton Beach underworld or what we call the bratva' . . . in Moscow if you are not connected, you don't do business . . . my family was connected . . . they were members of the Communist Party . . . through them, I was afforded entre' into their world . . . I knew who was real and understood the hierarchy . . . these relationships followed me through university and my career . . . I will tell you . . . I am a former KGB agent . . . I lived in their world. . . ."

Marisha set the stage and established her credentials as an authority on what she was about to say. I was shocked that she admitted to her KGB credentials, but it impressed the client and Sal.

Now to deliver the facts—not evidence or proof beyond any doubt, just the facts.

"So, who is Alexander Lithkov? . . . you heard my colleague describe his non-descript background . . . let me tell you who he is today . . . I will refer to him as Lithkov from here on . . . Lithkov is the frontman for Roman Illif . . . my family knew Illif in Russia . . . we knew of his connection to the bratva' . . . he was used by the Party to launder its money after the fall of the Soviet Union . . . but he was also used before the collapse to launder money . . . he was the Meyer Lansky of Russia . . . but much more violent . . . he killed at the behest of the Party and had his thugs kill . . . his reputation was more or less like that of John Gotti here in the United States . . . and he was trusted with the Party's money to do the right thing . . . he is not an oligarch . . . he is not one to get in the way of . . . distance is safety when it comes to Illif. . . ."

Marisha wisely used equivalent Mafia metaphors that the client would likely relate to. She was also telegraphing her multicultural understanding of the Mafia in the United States and mafia or bratva' in Russia. I could see that Sal was impressed with her delivery. Her KGB training taught her to tell a good story, even if she slightly mangled the facts. Bringing her to meet with the client was a stroke of genius. The optics were playing out just as expected.

"Now, Lithkov . . . Lithkov is what you here in America call a front . . . I would refer to him as a sleeper . . . he manages to stay below the radar . . . he is not well known or, for that matter, well regarded . . . or should I say, wasn't until he started investing in the taxi industry for Illif . . . Ilif saw the taxi industry as a golden opportunity to invest the Party's money . . . there were no serious impediments to purchasing medallions . . . setting up a shell company, preferably in Delaware or out west . . . starting buying medallions through the shell company . . . and then going after what you call the 'mother load' . . . get loans . . . that's where the real money is . . . use your existing medallions as collateral . . . pump up the value of the medallions . . . acquire more debt through additional loans . . . and when it all crashes, file for bankruptcy or walk away from the loans . . . the scheme was similar to the fuel tax scam by the Russians and the Mafia. . . ."

When Marisha mentioned this, I shuttered. Sal had represented several people involved in the fuel-tax scam. He was friends and family with the Columbo boss Anthony Pellegrino, who invested in this scam. Was this a shot across the bow by Marisha? It was hard to think it wasn't. Who knew, but did it matter? She did her homework and learned how the fuel tax scam worked. At this point, I had no choice but to let her sell due diligence. Marisha owned the stage, and me.

"Lithkov connections . . . and it's all about relationships in Moscow or Brighton Beach . . . you can ignore these relationships, but you do so at your peril . . . Lithkov is entrenched in Brighton Beach . . . he has met with Illif in Moscow . . . how do I know? . . . my people there told me where they met and provided me with specific dates and times . . . Lithkov has money buried in Jersey . . . I'm not referring to New Jersey . . . I'm referring to the Island of Jersey . . . there is an old idiom in the English language, 'birds of a feather flock together' . . . you can take it or leave it, but there is no question about it; Lithkov is laundering money for Illif. . . ."

Up until this meeting, Marisha had never shared this with me. Whether she winged it or made it up, her presentation was compelling. It was enough to have Sal take note and comment, "I'm not sure your client wants that on paper. . . ."

Sal understood the legal ramifications. So did the client. Perhaps not understanding the legal niceties, Marisha placed the client in an uncomfortable and legally-precarious position. They witnessed a *former* KGB agent telling the client his customer was a known money launderer.

So much for "we're in the business of making money, not chasing oligarchs." Plausible deniability just evaporated.

MEDALLION MAYHEM

Sal saw his opportunity to strike when I thought I'd be losing this well-heeled client. If the client retains Sal as his company's attorney, there may be a way to structure the loan to avoid legal entanglements with the government and protect the firm's assets. I was concerned that the client would suspect he was about to be fleeced.

Fortunately, Sal had developed a rapport with the client, and any ill thoughts were the furthest from the client's mind. All I could think about was the slippery slope had gotten even slipperier. Sal saw an opportunity; I saw more grief. For Sal, one person's grief is another person's opportunity.

The client also saw an opportunity. If Sal could structure the loan to Lithkov, this could also change the industry in New York and other cities.

The lending industry was changing, and Sal recognized that these changes would benefit the lenders and borrowers—the individual taxi drivers. They were able to obtain loans with virtually nothing down. Individual taxi drivers were encouraged by both the city and the lending institutions to apply for loans to own their medallions outright. It was the American dream repackaged. It was, in retrospect, a repeat of the 2008 financial crisis that saw the housing-mortgage market collapse.

Medallions were an asset they could borrow against as their equity artificially increased. Taxi drivers could use the medallion as collateral to purchase a house, send their children through college, or acquire any other asset.

The lending institution could distance itself from the taxi driver by extending broker's loans. Lithkov would encourage and solicit taxi drivers to take out interest-only loans. Lithkov could then comingle the monies he was receiving from Illif, washing the dirty money through an under-regulated financial institution.

Ultimately what Lithkov and others created was a giant Ponzi scheme. Those who got in early sold their medallions, recouped their investment, and made a healthy profit. Most drivers were left holding the bag—a medallion whose worth plummeted after Uber and Lyft entered the market.

Sal saw no downside to representing the client. The regulatory authorities would never investigate Lithkov; if he was, it was unlikely they would uncover anything that would preclude *our* client from lending to Lithkov. It was essentially risk-free, provided Lithkov made his payments to *our* client. A personal guarantee would protect *our* client.

Some would refer to the scheme as creative financing. It was genius. Everybody made money. The City in the fees charged for the medallions and the required taxes. The broker, Lithkov, cleaned Illif's money and made a percentage on the wash. The lending institution, *our* client, had a steady income stream. And the taxi driver who now *co-owned* an asset with the broker.

When the driver sought to refinance the loan, it amounted to a legal form of loansharking at one point, with an interest rate of 24%. And Sal would acquire all the collateral business that *our* client would derive from the industry. It was capitalism with a colossal *caveat emptor* attached. This new form of *creative financing* would revolutionize and reenergize a relatively dormant sector of the transportation industry in New York.

And no one was the wiser until the bubble burst. Lithkov's assets, those not secreted in foreign offshore accounts, were seized by *our* client's lending company. Taxi drivers were on the hook for millions of dollars in loans, which were impossible to repay. And city regulators blamed the lending institutions, the federal regulators, the brokers, and taxi drivers for engaging in irresponsible but not illegal practices. Predictably, the City feasted on the lower-level minions that worked 16 hours a day to achieve the American dream. The big guys were too big to fail.

Did Marisha get a sobering education on capitalism?

IT'S NEVER WHAT IT SEEMS

My due diligence in the taxi industry began quite innocently. A prospective borrower was suspected of being involved with the Russian mafia. I never thought I would end up in Brighton Beach conducting an undercover operation with Marisha.

Marisha had been off my radar for years. Other than infrequent phone calls, we hadn't collaborated on any investigations. She had now seen the sleazier aspects of money laundering.

My friend and colleague Sal had cashed in on the ancillary industry that fed off these predatory miscreants. Sal did nothing illegal, but whether it was moral is another question. Then again, much of what Sal did would not pass the smell test. But the rule of law is not society's moral compass.

A decade after investigating Lithkov, I learned of his predatory schemes in other large cities. Lithkov was not content making millions off the unsuspecting and disillusioned immigrant taxi drivers, many of whom filed for personal bankruptcy, fled back to the developing countries from whence they left, or committed suicide. The consequences of Lithkov's greed and avarice, while not witnessed by the average Joe or Jane citizen when they are transported from point A to point B, tell an appalling story about America and its *dream* or *nightmare*.

Ultimately Lithkov was exposed for the fraudster he was. Civil actions were filed demanding hundreds of millions of dollars. Much of it was forfeited or seized by the government for tax purposes.

Marisha and Matteo returned to Prague. We presented *our* client with a hefty invoice. Much like Maximillian, he didn't blink. He paid for it, no questions asked. We billed a drop in the bucket to what he recouped daily.

Sal and I remained friends. I still smoke his Cubans and savor his rarified cognacs. Sal was a defense attorney. He refused to take pedophiles, sex traffickers, and child molesters as clients. Financial criminals were within his scope of services and code of conduct. He never misled me on that issue.

My foray into this unseemly world of money laundering enlightened me about its destructive consequences.

Capitalism is a system based on the notion of fairness, meritocracy, and equitable distribution of resources.

What may, on the surface, appear to be a benign and harmless crime, money laundering, has been used to support terrorism, human enslavement, narcotics trafficking, and the illegal arms trade.

Worst of all, it silently corrodes capitalism and democracy. Elections manipulated through dirty money seem to be the latest KGB *modus operendi*. The evidence is staring us in the eyes every waking day.

If I learned only one lesson from this relatively brief interlude with the Russian *bratva'*, the upper world and underworld dance to the same *sound of music*.

No longer is corruption episodic or simply systemic. Strategic corruption, directed at critical targets, primarily the expansive media platforms, is now the weapon of choice. Fiction bleeds into reality. A litany of lies and deceptions infuses and defuses truth. Society has become cynical about what is "fake news" and what is "truth." And trust in our institutions of governance has been irrevocably weakened, at least for generations to come.

Perhaps we are now experiencing the creeping erosion of free-market democratic institutions, gradually replaced by a technologically-driven oligarchy. If so, the answer will require some bold and courageous decisions—not likely so long as money and greed contort our political leaders and processes.

EPILOGUE

By the 2000s, I was finished dealing with Russian oligarchs. It was not worth the sleepless nights, the deception that was part of the package, and the veiled dangers. It was only a matter of time before my ticket was punched. I continued "to keep my friends close, and my enemies closer" but focused more on the Asian market, particularly the exploding casino interests in Macau.

I began to travel more extensively throughout the Far East, soaking up a culture utterly alien to my thinking. As one indoctrinated with Western thought, I often questioned why the East and the West differed culturally and philosophically. It was an opportunity to re-visit my youthful years in California and my flirtation with Zen and Buddhism. It, too, proved to be yet another deep dive into a world steeped in darkness and mysterious rituals.

Fortunately, people like Sully de Fontaine and his cadre of investigators in the Far East supported my travels to Hong Kong and Macao. Bill and Luke, who worked in the financial industry, collectively educated me on the seamy banking business practices and what I would encounter.

Hong Kong was New York on steroids. The money that flowed in and out of Hong Kong was mind-boggling. Hong Kong had no housing crisis, except for those who could not afford the astronomical costs of the empty multi-million dollar apartments. Ghost cities are a shining tribute to the spoils of money laundering.

If Geneva and London were laundromats for the Russians, Hong Kong and Macau were car washes for the Chinese.

As I traveled throughout the Far East, I gradually realized that time had taken its toll. I could no longer conduct these investigations. The mental angst far outweighed the physical deterioration. Nothing was clean. Everything was murky and opaque. The upper world and the underworld were indistinguishable.

Enjoy all that this dirty money had to offer. Walk the magnificent Great Wall of China; visit the Forbidden City; vacation in Guangzhou, where the wealthy park their cash in multi-million dollar estates; sail Halong Bay and visit Phu Quoc Island; savor the hedonistic resorts in Phuket; explore and learn about the archaeological wonders of Angkor Watt; and paddle through the Mekong Delta, visiting families that lived relatively simple lives while their governments stole from them.

Just as I thought these worlds were a distant but unforgettable memory, I received a call from Marisha.

"Marty, I need a favor. My niece, a lawyer in Moscow, no longer wants to work in Russia. She graduated from an American law school . . . the University of North Carolina Law School. The war in Ukraine has soured her on Putin. . . . her future ambitions are in shambles . . . Do you think you can do something for her anywhere?"

"Marisha, you know I am always here for you . . . but can't Matteo do something for your niece?"

"Marty, Matteo, and I broke up months ago . . . I can't ask him for a favor . . . I thought of you immediately. . . ."

"Let me see what I can do . . . we'll talk later about your personal life. . . ."

Scouring my list of contacts, I reached out to colleagues in Germany. They knew of a company that might be searching for an attorney proficient in Russian and international law. The Russian/Ukraine war sanctions kicked in, and violations could prove costly.

Summoned to Baden-Baden, Germany, I traveled there to meet covertly with two *former* KGB agents and the individual, George, who would arrange for Marisha's niece to be interviewed by a multinational corporation headquartered in Vienna, Austria. Like others I had been in contact with earlier, George was intimately engaged in the financial machinations that camouflaged payments to Russian officials who demanded a piece of any company operating in Russia.

George had suggested that the three of us meet in the Friedrichsbad Baden-Baden. Immediately, I realized that George, as were the KGB agents, was wary of any surveillance conducted by German or American law enforcement or government officials. Here we would strip naked and discuss the role of Marisha's niece in this multinational corporation. It was again clear to me that the invisible hand was at work. After an hour of so discussion, we showered, dressed, and retreated to dinner at Schneider's Weinstube, where we reminisced about doing business in Russia during the Yeltsin era.

If there was one thing I had learned in my dealings with the KGB, remaining their friend was usually beneficial to all parties concerned. To operate in Russia, Marisha's niece would need a *roof*. These agents and George would be her *roof*, as would Marisha if she had not burnt her bridges.

After dinner, we found our way to the luxurious Baden-Baden Casino, where the KGB agents and George tried their luck at the roulette tables. I could only contemplate my earlier experiences with Max, Olga, and Marisha at Maxim's in London. This was the redux of London and Maximillian's foray into Russian investment and entrepreneurship. Nothing has changed other than a new set of players.

Retained to navigate the arcane laws of Russia and ensure that sanctions would not endanger this multinational corporation's assets, I inadvertently engineered yet another money-laundering scheme using Marisha's niece as a surrogate. Nothing in my career nor my life would have prepared me for being a part of this Machiavellian plot. The invisible hand once again and always prevails.

As for Marisha, we recollected how our relationship had come full circle. We were both on our own again. I knew that's how it had to be. Simply put, the minuses outweighed the pluses—a cold way of addressing what were once quite passionate emotions. I did not desire to re-enter her world—a world of duplicity, fraud, denial, and delusion. Marisha was a product of a warped and gilded environment. Then again, so was I. Life is messy. Serendipity plays a huge part in it.

Marisha reluctantly admitted, "Marty, you were right; the unassailable mistress is always present . . . I couldn't compete with it. . . ."

"And have you, Marisha, found your inner peace?"

"Marty, you told me, what makes me happy, can make me sad . . . I'm at peace with myself . . . I realize that there is more to life than the material things that made me happy at one time . . . I'm comfortable . . . maybe you'll come to Prague, or I'll go to New York? "

I left it an open question, knowing it would never end well.

As for Matteo, we remain good friends. We avoid talking about Marisha. Boundaries of privacy are respected. You can never mix business with pleasure. Matteo and Marisha learned that valuable lesson, as did Max.

Today, we witness a war in Ukraine that annihilates an entire culture and its people.

Vladimir Putin, the Godfather of the Kremlin, has reinforced that ugly caricature of the filthy, uncouth, savage Russian who has no regard for human rights.

Innocent people, women, children, and soon-to-be mothers who have done no wrong, sacrificed for the sadistic and vile expansionist vision of a low-level, evil former KGB officer.

The oligarchs have enabled Putin. They have blood on their hands. Their dirty money has finally caught up with the West. While the West is not paying near the price that Ukraine is, the economic fallout will be felt for many years and perhaps decades.

There is nothing victimless about money laundering.

And there is no *former* KGB, regardless of its name.

ACKNOWLEDGMENTS: TOO MANY AND TOO PERILOUS

Once again, Lawrence Knorr and Crystal Devine proved that skill and patience are the tools that make publishers and editors an incalculable asset to authors. Thank you!

To acknowledge the many others who in the words of Ernest Hemingway, made this unintended but remarkable journey "a moveable feast," out of caution, I will leave you nameless. We live in a world of international intrigue, global instability, leveraged kidnappings and imprisonment, and unsolved conspiratorial and strategic killings. The memories will never fade. Thanks to all who know who you are.

ABOUT THE AUTHOR

MARTIN REGINALD GRIMES is a renowned private investigator who has devoted a career investigating domestic and transnational organized crime. His investigations took him into the inner sanctums of Cosa Nostra, Latin and South American cartels, and Russian criminal networks synonymous with the KGB. Through his relationships with Russian oligarchs, Grimes is privy to some of the most intimate details of cross-border criminal enterprises, which inevitably involve money laundering, political corruption, extortion, and murder. *DARK FORCES* is a glimpse into this diabolical and duplicitous world, the results of which will be felt globally for many decades and likely forever.